GORDON M^CL

A Short

History *of the*

New Zealand

Wars

Bateman

Published in 2017 by David Bateman Ltd
30 Tarndale Grove, Albany, Auckland, New Zealand

www.batemanpublishing.co.nz

ISBN 978-1-86953-962-7

CREDITS:
Front cover — muskets, Te Papa Tongarewa, Wellington; shako/infantry hat
    — Puke Ariki, New Plymouth A 77.348
Back cover: top — Death of Major von Tempsky, Kennett Watkins,
    Alexander Turnbull Library, Wellington, C-033-006; bottom — Hone
    Heke and Eruera Patuone, George Angas, Alexander Turnbull Library,
    Wellington, PUBL-0014-01.

Book design: www.CVDgraphics.nz
Printed in China through Colorcraft Ltd, Hong Kong

Contents

New Zealand Wars Timeline
— Main events 1809–1883

1800s	1809	Ngati Uru kill and feast upon seventy of the crew of the *Boyd* and burn the vessel in Whangaroa Harbour. Whalers seek revenge but mistakenly kill innocent Maori.
	1819	Ngapuhi and Ngati Toa attack Taranaki and Whanganui iwi, heralding the Musket Wars of the following decade.
1820s	1820	Hongi Hika returns from England with about three hundred muskets and embarks on wars against southern iwi that start a killing spree and turbulence among iwi that lasts more than a decade.
1830s	1835	Ngati Mutunga and Ngati Tama originally from northern Taranaki invade the Chatham Islands and decimate or enslave the indigenous Moriori.
1840s	1840	Hone Heke Pokai is the first chief to sign the Treaty of Waitangi at the Bay of Islands on 6 February 1840.
	1841	After less than a year, the capital is moved from Okiato (Old Russell) to Auckland, irritating many Ngapuhi hapu.
	1843	A party of Nelson settlers attempt to arrest Ngati Toa chiefs, Te Rauparaha and Te Rangihaeata, at Wairau, Marlborough, over land disputes. Twenty-two settlers and four Maori die in a brief, bitter skirmish.
	1844	Hone Heke invades a blockhouse at Kororareka and cuts down the flagstaff carrying the British flag for the fourth time; Te Ruki Kawiti attacks the town to distract defences. The chiefs then sack the town, starting the War in the North: battles against British are fought at Puketutu, Ohaeawai and Ruapekapeka over the following two years. Maori win the first two but Ruapekapeka is indecisive.
	1846	A Ngati Toa taua (war party) attacks Boulcott's Farm in the Hutt Valley as iwi contest land ownership.

1850s	1858	Tainui leader, Te Wherowhero is chosen as the Maori king and takes the name Potatau I. This is seen by many settlers as a challenge to the sovereignty of Queen Victoria.
1860s	1860	Taranaki settlers try to buy a block of land on the Waitara River from an individual Maori, against the wishes of the senior Te Atiawa chief. A year-long war against British troops and settler militia ensues.
	1861	Wiremu Tamihana brokers a brief truce in Taranaki, but a renewed outbreak of conflict lasts on and off for most of the decade.
	1863	General Duncan Cameron, under the direction of Governor George Grey, moves across the Mangatawhiri River with his large army of British redcoats and the War in the Waikato begins. Meremere Pa is shelled by the British and evacuated by Maori who, in November, are defeated at the battle of Rangiriri.
	1864	After a series of battles across the Waikato, Maori resistance ends in the historic battle of Orakau, won after three days (on 2 April) by the British over hugely outnumbered Maori. The war moves to Bay of Plenty after British troops land at Tauranga and are defeated by Ngai-te-Rangi (supported by Ngati Koheriki warriors), led by Rawiri Puhirake. A few months later, Ngai Te Rangi were defeated building a pa at Te Ranga.
	1865	The capital moves from Auckland to Wellington and the government begins confiscating land from the 'rebels' — 1.215 million hectares in the Waikato, Bay of Plenty and Taranaki — under the Suppression of Rebellion Act passed in 1863.

1860s		
	1866	General Trevor Chute conducts a scorched-earth campaign in Taranaki with a regiment, some Forest Rangers and kupapa. He destroys villages and takes few prisoners. Te Kooti Arikirangi Te Turuki is exiled to the Chatham Islands without trial and founds his religion, Ringatu.
	1867	The Armed Constabulary was established as the settler population continued to grow quickly and the British government continued withdrawing its troops.
	1868	Ngati Ruanui leader Riwha Titokowaru defeats government forces in Taranaki and for several months has control of the province. The following year his troops desert him over a loss of personal mana. Te Kooti escapes from the Chathams aboard the *Rifleman*, with 295 men, women and children aboard and lands near Gisborne. By the end of the year, he controls most of Poverty Bay by force.
	1869	Te Kooti escapes from Ngatapa pa after it is stormed by government troops and kupapa, but many of his followers are captured and executed. Over the following months he conducts a series of brilliant guerrilla raids in the region before escaping to the Ureweras. Over the next few years he is constantly on the run.
1870s	1873	Te Kooti accepts King Tawhiao's pacifism and begins life in the King Country under the protection of Tawhiao and Rewi Maniapoto.
	1878	Te Whiti o Rongomai and Tohu Kakahi establish a centre of passive resistance at Parihaka, where Titokowaru also lives. Two thousand government troops invade the settlement in 1881. After three years of passive opposition to surveyor intrusions on their land, the leaders are arrested and imprisoned.
1880s	1883	Te Kooti is pardoned by the government but is not allowed to return to Poverty Bay because of local opposition. He is jailed briefly in 1889 for attempting a visit.

Introduction

I have on the wall of my office the framed, tattered, foxed remnant of a piece of silky fabric I was given by the government as a primary school pupil in 1940 to celebrate the centenary of the Treaty of Waitangi. It was headed:

NEW ZEALAND CENTENNIAL CELEBRATIONS SCHOOLS' DAY

The message it carried was: 'We want this day — 20th February, 1940 — to live in your memory not only as a wonderful holiday, but as a day of thanksgiving for all that has been achieved in New Zealand in the past one hundred years.

'Above all, we want this day to be an inspiration to you for the future. Soon after lunch you will hear from the platform a short address which should make you proud of our history and grateful for our priceless heritage. As you listen to it, we feel sure you will make up your mind to do your best in the future to prove yourself a good citizen of the Dominion, and of the Great British Empire to which we all belong.'

I can't remember what the short address was about. It was a long time ago. I guess the 'inspiring' message must have been pre-packaged and distributed well in advance to headmasters around the country and read out to schoolchildren around about the same time at special early afternoon assemblies. I hope the 'short address' contained something of what the Treaty was really about; but I doubt it.

I later heard a sentimentalised version of 'Rewi's Last Stand' and, at secondary school began to hear about the feats of courage by the Maori Battalion during the Second World War — as I learnt the European history on the school curriculum. It wasn't until I read Keith Sinclair's account of what he originally called the 'Land Wars' that I realised what the Treaty was about, that Maori fought extra battles in defence of their land and some political influence, and that thousands of professional British troops were brought in to suppress them.

I was bewildered and deeply annoyed that I could reach my twenties, having moved through the national education system, and been taught only the anglicised history of my country. I was also dismayed later again to work my way through the *Centennial Surveys*, eleven books published between 1939 and 1942, recounting the history of the previous century. They are predominantly a history of Pakeha New Zealanders . . . and that history was what two or three generations grew up with.

What I have tried to do here is to write a short, accessible story of the New Zealand wars in the hope that a wider range of people will gain some understanding of what happened here in the nineteenth century and build it into their understanding of who New Zealanders are and where we have failed and where we have triumphed. I hope many readers will move on to a deeper knowledge of the nineteenth century that helped shape us as a nation. This will be found among the books I have listed in the bibliography.

Without sincere respect for the past, we remain rootless in the present and flounder towards the future. 'The most effective way to destroy people,' wrote George Orwell, 'is to destroy and obliterate their own understanding of their history.' Fortunately, Maori and recent New Zealand scholars have been too strong to let that happen.

Chapter 1
The Wars in Context

The New Zealand Wars can only be seen clearly in the context of their time. First, they came in the aftermath of dreadful losses of life that Maori inflicted upon themselves during what have been called the Musket Wars of the 1820s.

Secondly, the British Empire was at the peak of its power in the nineteenth century and its leaders had a mindset that they were not plundering the countries they invaded but mainly spreading trade and modern civilisation to the benefit of all. The sun never set on this empire, we were taught in the twentieth century at home in our part of the 'old Commonwealth' — the white people part that managed for a century to whitewash its past as well. Indeed, the sun never rose again on some parts of the empire after the British arrived.

The first clashes between Maori and Pakeha were explosive but brief: in Golden Bay between local Maori (Ngati Tumatakokiri) and the Dutch East Indies expedition led by Abel Janszoon Tasman, in two vessels, the *Heemskerck* and the *Zeehaen*, in 1642; and at contact points after the arrival of James Cook in the *Endeavour* a hundred and twenty-seven years later. Serious early-contact conflict also occurred between Maori and French explorers in the Bay of Islands: Jean de Surville at the end of 1769 in a clash with Ngapuhi; and Marion Du Fresne three years later in a tragic massacre by Ngare Raumati.

The most serious fighting between Maori and Pakeha before the signing of the Treaty occurred in Whangaroa Harbour in 1809, when Ngati Uru, the local iwi (tribe), killed and feasted on the seventy crew (some few escaped) aboard the cargo vessel, *Boyd*, and burnt the ship. It was an act of utu against the treatment of a young Maori chief, Te Ara, who had been punished during the trip from Sydney. European whalers immediately sought their own utu, killing many local Maori, although at Te Pahi's pa in the Bay of Islands and not the Whangaroa people responsible. Te Pahi had arrived at the scene after the massacre and attempted to rescue some of the Europeans still alive but the whalers were convinced he and his people were guilty. The killing, and particularly the cannibalism, halted trade for several years as Europeans avoided the country and it delayed the establishment of Samuel Marsden's Christian mission until 1814.

Cook's four visits were soon followed by convict settlements in Australia, and the arrival of whalers and sealers in the Bay of Islands. A trade with Maori soon began in muskets, a new and lethal weapon that seemed a gift to a warrior people who had long fought among themselves in brutal enough encounters over land or fishing rights or over utu — redress for past slights, both small and grave. Previously these battles had been hand-to-hand encounters with patu (clubs) and taiaha (a staff spear). Casualties were limited by the nature of the weapons. And the fights were seasonal with the need for periods of planting and harvesting.

But now, the new and prolific potato as well as maize meant wars need not be strictly seasonal, supplies of food could be carried by warrior bands, and the wars could be prolonged, lethal and sweep over large distances. The effect of the first muskets was largely indecisive but when Hongi Hika arrived back from a visit to England in 1821 with three hundred of them, the wars began in earnest with Hongi's Ngapuhi the first iwi to decimate old enemies — Ngati Whatua. Population growth and increasing pressure on resources had already exacerbated inter-tribal tensions but muskets made these tensions explode into terrible and far-reaching wars. The result, during the 1820s and the early 1830s, was thousands of dead and whole iwi dispersed as they fled from their traditional land holdings.

Early battles were fought by Ngati Whatua against the invading Ngapuhi and Waikato. They were defending their favoured pa site atop the volcanic cone in the Auckland Domain — a place they called Pukekawa, 'Hill of Bitter Memories'. A totara growing in the cone marks the final reconciliation between Ngati Whatua and Waikato in 1828, both peoples bowed down by war weariness.

The wars spread through the country and Maori nearly destroyed themselves as a people. The death toll has been put at between sixteen and eighteen thousand in a population that was estimated at somewhere near a hundred thousand before the wars began. But it can only be a guess. By the time the Treaty was signed traditional land ownership had become confused because of the dispersal of iwi, a factor in the land battles in Taranaki. The war weariness among Maori may have made them more inclined to sign the Treaty. When William Hobson moved the capital from Russell to Auckland in 1841, he was welcomed by Ngati Whatua to an isthmus that had once been a thriving almost urban settlement and was now almost empty. Local Maori counted on the British presence to give them protection.

The story of these internecine wars and their scale seemed put aside from New Zealand history during most of the nineteenth and twentieth centuries because that history was written by Pakeha, but the huge loss of life had an impact on the New Zealand Wars of the next generation.

From the fifteenth to the nineteenth centuries, European countries invaded, materially exploited, and declared they would 'civilise' the 'savages' or 'barbarians' in almost every Asian and African country. And among all the European colonisers still rampaging around the world in the eighteenth and nineteenth centuries, Britain was at the forefront with the biggest navy able to control the seas and carry its highly experienced and skilled troops to flashpoints as required.

As Maori began to repulse settlers' attempts to buy or confiscate their land within five years of the Treaty of Waitangi being signed, gradually increasing numbers of British redcoats were shipped in to ensure that New Zealand became an orderly replica of England.

The Treaty of Waitangi was not a one-off. The British signed treaties with indigenous people in a number of the countries they effectively invaded. All were quickly transgressed as the demand for land or profitable resources overcame what may have been good intentions.

The treaties became a useful temporising device for subduing indigenous resistance to invasion by Europeans. At about the same time thousands of British troops were suppressing Maori ambitions for land and political influence, American Indians were in retreat across the United States from the great western surge of land-hungry easterners and immigrants. The process was similar: a treaty with the indigenous inhabitants; pressure build-up to find land for settlers; abrogation of the treaty; a military offensive and the removal of the Indians from their ancestral lands either further west or to reservations in less salubrious locations.

There were only about two thousand Europeans living in New Zealand when the Treaty was signed. Few were typical of the flood of settlers, mostly in organised groups, that came in over the following three decades. It doesn't require a great leap of the imagination to understand that Maori appreciated the great material advantages the early arrivals brought with them. The Polynesians would have arrived here in the late thirteenth century with many tropical fruits from their departure point and their disillusionment would have been shattering when they found none but the kumara, the gourd and taro would grow in this temperate climate and in many places they were marginal.

So it's no surprise that potatoes, peaches, maize, apples and other temperate fruits and vegetables, not to mention metals, cotton and wool, were boons beyond the dreams of its long-time inhabitants. They quickly learnt to cultivate them and to trade with the early European visitors who were themselves trading in whales, seals and timber. Maori gardens kept the earliest immigrants alive and well fed. But it was one thing to bring these gifts from the northern hemisphere and another to want to take over all the land they grew in.

It's important to get inside the British mind at the time. Even liberal thinkers were convinced that those people outside central Europe were 'savages' or 'barbarians' and the duty of colonisers was not just to create beneficial trade but to 'civilise' the 'natives' with moral and religious crusades. Become Christians, adhere to our rules for justice and order . . . or else.

In some of the European colonies, the exploitation following invasion was so unvarnished, the colonising organisation was a corporation or a Christian religious order crusading to convert the heathen. In India, for example, the East India Company ruled the country for most of a century, with the complicity of Indians under the command of soldiers provided by the British government to support the corporation. That ended with what was known at the time as the 'Indian Mutiny' in 1857–58, but which is now known in India as the first Indian war of independence. It was an explosive rebellion by Indians who killed British soldiers, public servants, murdered many of their families, and raped a number of British women.

The rebellion was put down with shameless brutality. Some 'rebel' leaders were strapped over the mouths of cannons and blown to pieces. An estimated one hundred thousand Indians died in the period of the coloniser's response. Among the British units involved in that savage retribution were the 43rd (Monmouthshire) Regiment of Foot and the 68th (Durham) Regiment of Foot, both of which were then shipped here to fight Maori in the New Zealand Wars. The 57th (West Middlesex) Regiment was moved to India at the time, but apparently was too late to take part and moved on to this country. Most of the British troops were shipped in from New South Wales.

To understand how even liberal, individual English thinkers such as John Ruskin saw the British as inherently superior to other races, it is instructive to read his account in a lecture as the crisis in India developed. Ruskin was an eminent and influential art critic and liberal reformer. At the height of the 'Indian Mutiny', he wrote that he had recently been to Scotland and felt 'a peculiar painfulness in its scenery, caused by the non-manifestation of human art'. He said it was the first time in his life he had been in any country possessing no valuable monuments or examples of art. However, of the models throughout Britain for the teaching of design, 'there are, I suppose, none in their kind, more admirable than the decorated works of India'.

So, 'On the one side you have a race rejoicing in art, and eminently and universally endowed with the gift of it; on the other you have a people careless of art, and apparently incapable of it . . . '

What, he asked next, was the effect on the moral character of each nation — whether 'those rude chequers of the tartan, or the exquisitely fancied involutions of the Cashmere, fold habitually over the noblest hearts?' Well, the Indians, it turns out, may be consummate artists but they were guilty of 'cruelty stretched to its fiercest against the gentle and unoffending, and corruption festered to its loathsomest in the midst of a witnessing presence of a disciplined civilization'.

This exuberant justification of the armed exploitation

of another country ends with: 'Out of the peat cottage come faith, courage, self-sacrifice, purity and piety, and whatever else is fruitful in the work of Heaven; out of the ivory palace come treachery, cruelty, cowardice, idolatry, bestiality, — whatever else is fruitful in the work of Hell.'

In one speech, Ruskin, the most notable English art critic of his time, had, in defence of his 'civilization', repudiated any possible moral influence for the good from art.

Given the gift of food plants from the northern hemisphere, there is some irony in the fact that, briefly during the 1840s and more unrelentingly in the 1860s, Maori fought to preserve land in areas where they had most successfully adapted temperate-zone food plants. They were bewildered by the almost total disregard for their land and chiefly authority they thought they had been assured by the Treaty; while their opponents insisted that, because the Treaty gave Queen Victoria sovereignty, Maori were subject to British law and order. Some of Maori's friends and defenders — Chief Justice Sir William Martin, among others — noted that British law and order should have entitled them to go to courts on land issues.

It is important to remember, when recounting this appetite for land, that not only Maori and most indigenous people had a reverential attitude towards the land on which they based their living economy and had probably fought to gain or retain, European settlers also sought it with deep emotional need. Where they came from, land ownership was associated with status and security. In Britain, the great hope for ordinary people to gain the status of yeoman was through the ownership of even a small plot of land. For the earliest settlers, it was often what they emigrated for after being dispossessed by the enclosures in England and the clearances in Scotland. And, at least until the 1980s, owning your own plot was an emotional need for most New Zealanders.

The context of the post-wars century was to blame Maori, praise their pointless courage as an historical aside, and try to ignore events that shaped our nation's future. The confiscation and resale of Maori land was seen as a way to mitigate the large national debt that was a consequence of the British army intervention. *The Spectator* in London carried a story in January 1864, and reproduced in Auckland's *Daily Southern Cross* in April, which extols 'something of a Roman' project, which endorsed a plan to settle twenty thousand men, backed by a loan of £2,500,000, in military villages 'so distributed' in the North Island that 'they will constitute a complete and well-knit system of defence, segregate the natives, and cover the country with cultivation . . . By some such process alone can the Maori race be saved from extinction.

'What the colonists desire is the cessation, not only of war, but of the fear of war, with the savage iwi on the fringes of whose far-spreading but desolate lands they dwell. They have tried the laissez-aller method; they have tried empirical plans of conciliation and nursing; both have failed. Neither non-intervention nor the bribes of Sir George Grey have sufficed to raise the Maoris to that state which we call civilisation, and which would render the land habitable.

'The Maoris have imbibed a notion that it is practicable to set up a Maori kingdom self-governed and independent, and for this they are fighting . . . No Maori kingdom imaginable could limit the growth of a British colony. Persistence in the Maori idea means perpetual war, and perpetual war means extermination, sooner or later, of the Maori race.'

What happened after the denouement of the wars that ended in the 1870s was that Pakeha, in general, simply wanted the whole business to fade away. They had won. Maori had lost. Our history gave the losers a metaphorical pat on the head, and the 'winners' got on with their racist colonial lives.

Alan E. Mulgan was born in 1881 at Katikati into one of the families of Irish Protestant farmers who migrated in a group in 1875 and had the capital to set themselves up in the Bay of Plenty area. His father E. K. Mulgan quickly abandoned farming and ended his career as a senior inspector of schools. Alan became one of the most influential journalists, writers and broadcasters in the first half of the twentieth century, and his work was a reflection of the prevailing New Zealand ethos of his time.

He was a kind and pleasant man but an inveterate sentimentalist and nostalgist in conversation and in almost everything he wrote about New Zealand and its history. In 1925, he summed up the period after the wars with: 'The country, which in 1870 had a white population of a quarter of a million was saddled with a debt. The Maoris who had rebelled were, in their anger, sullen and without hope. They had tried the Christianity and the civilization brought by the white men, and these had failed them.

'Fortunately, however, though the wars set back the work of adapting the Maori to new conditions, in only one or two iwi was the resentment permanent. A wise policy of leniency and patience won back friendship. The rights granted by the Treaty of Waitangi were not taken away. The Maori was given separate representation in Parliament. The opening up of the country gradually broke down the barriers and sense of wrong, and Maori and white man lived in friendship side by side.' He added that an English statesman, who had left the colony early on and thought Maori 'doomed', found when he returned decades later that the two races were living 'in perfect harmony'.

Alan and his father wrote a book called *The New Zealand Citizen*, aimed at young readers. First published during the First World War, it was reissued regularly for at least ten years. It casts an unremitting gloss on Britain, or rather England. In a chapter headed 'Causes of British Success', the Mulgans wrote: 'We can say of the Englishman that he has a special talent for governing, and his ideal of government has been one that, while preserving order and sternly punishing wrong-doing, allows citizens a great deal of personal freedom. This talent includes an unrivalled ability to govern subject races, by which is meant the millions of coloured people of various nationalities and religions who live within the Empire, but have not a full share, or any share at all, in government.

'Many wars have been waged to subdue such peoples, and with respect to some of them, British authority is still based on force. But if British officials have not gained the affection of such people, they have won their trust and respect. Certain native races who would probably attack their British masters if they could do so with good hope of success, respect British honour and justice . . .'

In a chapter on immigration, *The New Zealand Citizen*, includes: 'We want immigrants, but we do not want everybody. We do not want the destitute, the criminal, or people belonging to the coloured races. The experience of the United States of America, where millions of negroes and people of mixed race form one of the gravest social and political problems of our time, has made us determined to keep New Zealand white, though we make an exception in the case of the Maoris, whom we treat as equals and admit to citizenship.

'It would take too long to tell you why we keep out people belonging to coloured races, save to say that it is a question of ways of living and ideals, besides, of course, the desire to keep the blood of our people pure. Some of the peoples we exclude have many fine qualities, and possess a civilization and a culture older than our own.'

Elsewhere, he wrote that Sir George Grey 'strove to keep the peace, but he was obliged to take measures to defend the Europeans against the menacing King movement in the Waikato'; and like almost all the twentieth-century commentators, the British missteps against Maori are 'blunders' made by people of goodwill.

And so on. It was not that the Mulgans were extreme in their views but, rather, representative of attitudes of their time. Lindsay Buick in his 1926 book, *The Rebellion of Hone Heke*, wrote that the issue was 'more than the mere question of the Government buying land from the natives and selling it to the Europeans. They were, in fact, largely the outcome of that inherent conflict which must ever wage between the forces of barbarism and those of civilization: the inevitable fear and apprehension of the savage are the breaking-down of his old customs by the introduction of civilized law.

'This fear, aggravated by the forces of envy, of national jealousy, and all uncharitableness inseparable from the founding of a colony such as New Zealand, if persisted in, could have but one result and but one remedy — an appeal to arms.' He goes on to say in this introduction that 'the primitive mind of the Maori could but dimly comprehend' the establishment of 'constitutional Government'.

Similar is the tone of A. H. Reed's *The Story of New Zealand*, which sold about eleven thousand copies in five editions between 1945 and 1950. The wars are dealt with as a kind of side issue to the real history of the country. Again, Maori are praised for their courage in battle but not their acumen or the validity of their cause. Only James Cowan, who often wrote with too much exuberance and heightened colour but was a good reporter, gives much depth of humanity to Maori and their traditions.

The long-lasting paternalism and historical amnesia pretended the New Zealand Wars were a blip in our glorious national story instead of a continuum over many decades. In his *Maori and Pakeha: A History of New Zealand*, published in 1921, Alan Mulgan, after acknowledging the 'blunder of the Waitara purchase', moves on to write: 'It was twenty years since the signing of the Treaty of Waitangi, in which a savage race acknowledged the "sovereignty" of one highly civilized . . . It was an old story, always a problem and often a tragedy, of the clash between civilized and uncivilized races. It was the inevitable conflict, which could have but one end, between the strong who wished to expand and the weak who wished to hold on to more than they could use, and saw their ancient nationality threatened with submersion by an alien people'.

He then continues by deprecating 'the irritating and

sometimes offensive attitude, born of ignorance and prejudice, displayed by many colonists towards a proud and sensitive race. To such men the finest of savages were simply "niggers".' And in reporting the wars in Taranaki and Waikato, Mulgan does try to be fair, if always paternalistic towards Maori. But the same frame of mind is there; referring to casualties in a Taranaki war encounter he reports, 'Two men were injured on our side'. In his novel, *Spur of Morning* (1934) he does create a picture of how New Zealand was pulling away somewhat from the tight embrace of English culture.

By 1958, when he was in his late seventies, Alan Mulgan had at last gained an understanding of how our history had been misused. He wrote in his engaging memoir, *The Making of a New Zealander*: 'In a vague way we knew there had been Maori wars . . . This had been so-called rebel country, but the local Maoris gave no trouble. We were taught no New Zealand history, at home or at school, and this was so also when I went to school in Auckland. Another significant thing was this: I was in Tauranga more than once in my teens, and no one thought of taking me to see the old Mission House, which is at one end of the town, or the site of the Gate Pa fight at the other.'

In the last quarter of the nineteenth century some influential Maori were born, educated at 'native schools'

and moved on to Te Aute College, a prestigious secondary school for Maori boys. The most famous was Apirana Turupa Ngata, who gained a law degree and became a member of the high establishment with a long career as an MP and Cabinet Minister. Ngata did a great deal to raise the profile of anglicised Maori, adapted to Pakeha ways, and worked hard on the consolidation and development of land still held by Maori.

He was Ngati Porou, an East Cape iwi that had escaped confiscation of its land and dire consequences after the New Zealand Wars. He was a symbol of racial harmony and adaptability at a time when absorption was the theme of Maori and Pakeha politics. Maori schoolchildren were sharply discouraged from speaking Te Reo.

Ngata would have been aware that in 1877 the Chief Justice Sir James Prendergast's ruling on a case involving land ownership between Ngati Toa and the Anglican church said the court could not consider claims involving native title. Because such claims were based on the Treaty of Waitangi, they were 'worthless'. The Treaty, he declared, had been signed by representatives of a 'civilised nation and a group of savages' who were not capable of understanding it. He added that the Treaty was a 'nullity' because it had not been incorporated in law.

In 1922, a time when historians were pretending that the fight to civilise the savages had been won and the New Zealand Wars were an aberration best glossed over, Ngata wrote an 'explanation' of the Treaty in Maori, 'published for the Maori Purposes Fund Board'. It said the Treaty placed in the hands of the Queen of England 'sovereignty and the authority to make laws. Some sections of the Maori people violated that authority. War arose from this and blood was spilled. The law came into operation and land was taken in payment. This itself was a Maori custom — revenge, plunder to avenge a wrong.'

An extraordinary statement from a lawyer. Maori were to abide by British law, but in the case of land confiscation Maori custom is invoked to justify it.

He wound up by saying he had been lengthy in his explanation but 'It could have been quite short if I had just stated, the Treaty of Waitangi created Parliament to make laws. The Treaty has given us the Maori Land Court with all its activities. The Treaty confirmed Government purchases of lands which is still being done and it also confirmed past confiscations. The Treaty sanctioned the levying of rates and taxes on Maori lands, it made one law for the Maori and the Pakeha. If you think these things are wrong and bad then blame our ancestors who gave away their rights in the days when they were powerful.'

Beneath the quiet congratulations all round on how Maori had adapted and been civilised within a British colony ran an undercurrent of racism based on national paranoia. 'Mother England', as it was still frequently referred to until after the Second World War, was half a world away as, like Australia, we lived under the perceived looming threat of high-population Asian countries and Russia further north. The innovative and radical Liberal government of the 1890s was led by Richard Seddon, who was an intensely emotional supporter of the British Empire as it fought to dispossess the Boers in South Africa where it established the modern world's first concentration camps. In 1903, during a journey around the South Pacific, Seddon told Cook Islanders they would be better off having the bubonic plague than a Chinese immigrant.

In August 1908, the United States Pacific fleet arrived in Auckland. Known as 'The Great White Fleet', it had been dispatched by the first seriously imperialist United States President, Theodore Roosevelt, to demonstrate American sea power to the world. Auckland city's population was just over forty thousand but, as Auckland chief librarian, John Barr, wrote in his 1922 history: 'The fleet reached Auckland on Sunday morning, August 9th, and the Admiral [Rear-Admiral Charles Sperry] and his men were welcomed by crowds estimated at 100,000 persons, who utilised every vantage point on the harbour front . . .

'Thereafter a week of festivities, the like of which the city had never previously indulged in, took place, including banquets, receptions on land and aboard the ships of the fleet, reviews, race meetings and sports, both general and aquatic.'

The Prime Minister, Joseph Ward, and most Members

of Parliament came up from Wellington for the occasion. A hardcover book of two hundred and seventy pages, written by James Cowan, extolling the virtues of New Zealand, was published and given freely to the visitors. The introductory 'Our Greeting to the Fleet', written by the Prime Minister, said: 'Today there rises in our breasts a special pride in our old Anglo-Saxon race, for are you not a branch of that great tree which has spread from clime to clime to raise the level of the world's civilization? We are but an Island people, young in years, few in numbers, but rich in hope and strong in will to preserve the honour and traditions of our race . . .

'The armaments of America, and above all, her navy, are but majestic instruments for working out the aims of higher civilisation. Your fleet stands for peace not war — for justice not aggression — for freedom not tyranny.'

How Major Dion Williams, of the United States Marine Corps, must have smiled as he read these cringing words, working as he was on the 'The Naval War Plan for the Attack on Auckland, New Zealand', an extraordinarily detailed invasion plan released in Washington DC forty years later.

By the middle of the twentieth century our history had disappeared under a 'Britain of the South' myth: more English than England, more liberal, egalitarian and enlightened than the Mother Country, a white history, with paternalistic references to Maori if any references were made at all. What little New Zealand history that was taught in schools and universities was history on a road without the bumps of Maori confiscations and chilling racism.

It wasn't until late in the 1950s that scholar Keith Sinclair began to examine primary sources and tell the story of those decades of conflict in the nineteenth century. He has been followed by a succession of writers, most meticulously and thoughtfully James Belich, whose focused examination of the New Zealand Wars has been a revelation to modern New Zealanders. It's not that the scholars have revised our history, they have disinterred it. But in many ways, we owe the resurrection of our story to the Maori renaissance that began in the 1970s when young, educated Maori refused to be silenced and, at last, a government listened.

Chapter 2
The Cook Strait Settlements

In 1840, when the Treaty was signed, there were about two thousand Europeans in New Zealand, almost all of them involved in the extraction industries: whales, seals, timber (mainly kauri for ships' spars) and flax for cordage. But once the Treaty was signed and the country became a colony, Maori became British citizens and British citizens automatically became New Zealand citizens.

In Britain, there was mass unemployment as a result of the Industrial Revolution, the dispossession of land from enclosures in England and Scotland, and famine drove people from Ireland. The millions who emigrated mostly took the relatively easy ride across the Atlantic to the United States or Canada. For most, the expensive and arduous four or five months in a sailing ship to the other side of the world, to New Zealand, was not an option — neither affordable nor desirable. Yet the European population here rose from that two thousand to thirty thousand by the early 1850s and more than a hundred thousand by the end of that decade, easily outnumbering Maori.

Most of the settlers in the 1840s were enticed here by the New Zealand Company, set up in London to promote idealised English communities in Wellington, Nelson, Whanganui and New Plymouth, settlements in a country promoted as 'the Britain of the South'. (Both countries are in a temperate zone and much the same size: New Zealand marginally smaller than the British Isles.)

A short time before war was seriously disturbing Northland, skirmishes were occurring in Marlborough, Wellington and the Hutt Valley, and Whanganui. The more prolonged and intense war in Taranaki came later. All the conflict in the Cook Strait settlements revolved around land disputes between Pakeha and Maori, which also exacerbated some Maori inter-tribal enmities. The company claimed it had legitimately bought land around this region, initially through an advance party that arrived before the main body of immigrants left England and before the signing of the Treaty. After the settlers arrived in Wellington, they bought land for satellite settlements in the Hutt Valley, at Whanganui and Nelson/Marlborough.

The problems over land ownership and political control were compounded during the 1840s by three factors. One was renewed claims for traditional tribal land by Maori iwi that had been dispersed during the Musket Wars of the 1820s and 1830s. Another was the sense of righteousness by many English settlers who saw their planned settlements as an enhanced extension of the English way of life and its legal and political system and which did not factor in Maori rights. The third was the aggressive push against any Maori resistance by the new Governor, George Grey, who was aware of the bitter settler resentment against his predecessor Robert FitzRoy for his judgement on the Wairau Affray. Effigies of FitzRoy were burnt in the streets of Wellington.

FitzRoy was a member of an old, distinguished aristocratic family and attended the Royal Naval College before going to sea at the age of fourteen in 1819. He rose to command the *Beagle* which carried Charles Darwin as the naturalist on an expedition that visited the Bay of Islands in 1835. He contributed to the three-volume account of the expedition and was awarded a gold medal by the Royal Geographical Society. He became second Governor of New Zealand in 1843 on the death of William Hobson and held the position until late in 1845.

For Grey, it was easier to be more aggressive in the south where Maori were not as numerous, especially with his gradually increasing British military support.

The Wairau Affray, called for a long time the 'Wairau Massacre', occurred in June 1843 and was the country's first armed clash between Maori and settlers. Captain Arthur Wakefield with a party of fifty armed men, including a police magistrate, Augustus Thompson, moved   into the Wairau Valley to arrest chiefs Te Rauparaha and Te Rangihaeata on a warrant for taking action against a survey party on land whose sale to Pakeha was disputed by Maori. Apparently, a member of Wakefield's party fired a shot by accident and in the following eruption of shooting Te Rangihaeata's wife was killed. He demanded utu and by the end of the affray, Wakefield and twenty-one of his men lay dead. Four Maori also died.

Governor FitzRoy investigated and found the settlers were in the wrong because the land was legally in dispute and the warrant was, therefore, at least injudicious. It was a decision backed by the Attorney-General William Swainson. But the settlers in the new New Zealand Company towns were outraged that the Maori involved went unpunished.

Skirmishes then exploded in the Hutt Valley in May 1846. Grey was brutal in his response to Maori land claims after Te Rangihaeata led his Ngati Toa people against European settlement on land they considered still in dispute. Ngati Toa were supported in their opposition to settlement by Te Mamaku from Whanganui with his Ngati Haua-te-rangi warriors. But they were opposed by Ngati Awa, loyal to the British at that time, who joined a raiding party attempting to capture Te Rangihaeata at his pa in Pauatahanui. They found the pa had been abandoned. However, they captured a minor chief who had come south with Te Mamaku, court-martialled him for 'rebellion' and hanged him.

As a gesture signifying his power but which later seemed futile, Grey then arrested Te Rauparaha who, despite his former association with Te Rangihaeata, had played no part in the Hutt skirmishes.

The fiercest confrontation in the Hutt Valley was the battle of Boulcott's Farm, which became legendary after fifty men of the 58th Regiment in a stockade valiantly held off an assault by an estimated two hundred Maori. Six soldiers, two other Europeans and an unknown number of Maori died. A bugler sounded the alarm to warn his colleagues of the surprise attack. Struck on the right shoulder, he shifted the bugle to his left hand before he was axed to death. The battle was a minor event in the context of the serious battles between Maori and Pakeha over the following twenty-four years but the embellished story of William Allen, the boy bugler (he was probably twenty-one) who died trying to save the lives of his fellow soldiers fitted snugly into the mythology of the British Empire and has lingered a long time in the history of Wellington.

Whanganui, close to the mouth of the Whanganui River, was a New Zealand Company satellite settlement set up with a sixteen thousand-hectare purchase. From its beginning until 1854 the settlement was called Petre after Baron Petre, a London director of the New Zealand Company. (A more recent name dispute followed a move to change the spelling from long-time 'Wanganui' to 'Whanganui', the choice of which remains optional.) The river was an important transport route between the central North Island and the west coast for Maori and also for Pakeha in the early days of settlement. At 290 kilometres from its source on Mt Tongariro to the sea, it is the third-longest river in the country, after the Waikato and Otago's Clutha.

Maori in the fertile southern stretch of the river were generally in support of settlement near the river mouth but the upper-river Maori, led by Te Mamaku — the chief and his warriors involved in the Hutt Valley and Pauatahanui skirmishes — were concerned at the scale of the arrivals.

About four months after the signing of the Treaty, company agent Edward Jerningham Wakefield had paid an estimated £700 for the sixteen thousand hectares around the river mouth. When the purchase was disputed by some Maori four years later, Land Commissioner William Spain, who had been involved in land issues in the Hutt Valley, ruled against the company but said that, as the settlers had acted in good faith, the company should make good with further payments. It was an obscure and indecisive ruling that did nothing to settle the issue. An assurance from Te Mamaku, that the settlers were not at risk as long as no soldiers were brought in, was ignored.

With the example of the Hutt Valley skirmish a few months before and the knowledge that Te Mamaku had been involved, the Whanganui settlers, outnumbered by the region's Maori, welcomed a decision by Grey to send in British soldiers to form a garrison town. The troops from the 58th Rutlandshire Regiment arrived late in 1846 aboard HMS *Calliope*, accompanied by the Government brig, *Victoria*, and a gunboat, with a swivel gun, that could operate freely on the river. The troops mounted two twelve-pound guns in a large stockade on the hill that commands the town.

In May 1847, the murder of a settler's wife and children on their farm panicked the community but local Maori brought in five of the suspects and handed them over to the soldiers. Four were hanged and one released because of his young age. This was followed quickly by Te Mamaku setting up a blockade, and one foray into the edge of the town led to casualties on both sides — two British soldiers killed, eleven wounded, and three Maori dead, ten wounded. After three months, Te Mamaku withdrew to his pa further north.

These skirmishes may not have been battles on the scale of those that followed in Taranaki, Waikato and Bay of Plenty but they were not forgotten. In Wellington, arguments over the placement of memorials for the battle of Boulcott's Farm continued until well into the twentieth century.

In May 1864, a war party of three hundred Pai Marire ('Hauhau') followers descended from the upper reaches of the Whanganui River to attack the town. They were stopped at Moutoa Island by kupapa (Maori who, for a variety of reasons and with various levels of commitment, fought on the side of the government) in a fierce half-hour battle that cost about seventy lives. Pai Marire was a Christian sect within a Maori cultural setting, some groups of which were taken over by members violently opposed to land sales.

Eighteen months after the Moutoa Island battle, grateful Whanganui citizens (apart from one or two racist ranters) put up a memorial to the warriors who lost their lives in the battle to save the town. The memorial's inscription referred to the Pai Marire attackers as 'fanatics and barbarians'.

'A couple of memorials' in the town offended the great American writer, Mark Twain, when he visited in the 1890s. In his *More Tramps Abroad*, an account of a world tour at the end of the 1890s, which included a visit to New Zealand, he wrote:

'One is in honour of white men "who fell in defence of law and order against fanaticism and barbarism". Fanaticism . . . If you carve it at Thermopylae . . . or upon Bunker Hill monument, and read it again — "who fell in defence of law and order against fanaticism you will perceive what the word means and how mis-chosen it is. Patriotism is patriotism. Calling it fanaticism cannot degrade it . . . It is right to praise those brave white men who fell in the Maori war — they deserve it; but the presence of that word detracts from the dignity of their cause and their deeds, and makes them appear to have spilt blood in a conflict with ignoble men, men not worthy of that costly sacrifice.

'But the men were worthy. It was no shame to fight them. They fought for their home, they fought for their country; they bravely fought and bravely fell; and it would take nothing from the honour of the brave Englishmen who lie under the monument, but add to it, to say that they died in defence of English law and English homes against men worthy of the sacrifice — the Maori patriots.'

These were serious local skirmishes over New Zealand Company land that pitted Maori against settler and Maori against Maori, but in the context of the New Zealand Wars they were largely inconsequential. The land disputes in Taranaki were the sparks that set off the major wars of the 1860s.

Chapter 3
War in the North

*I*n July 1844, Hone Heke Pokai and his men cut down the flagstaff on Maiki Hill in Kororareka. Heke had provided the mast for the Maori flag but now it was flying the Union Jack, a symbol that, he had decided, represented oppression against Maori chiefly authority: rangatiratanga.

The Governor, Robert FitzRoy, foreseeing what he considered continued aggression from this troublesome man and not knowing quite how much support he had, sent to New South Wales for military reinforcements. After a meeting between Heke and Hokianga rangatira Tamati Waka Nene convened by Church of England head, Bishop George Selwyn, Heke wrote a letter to FitzRoy that seemed to profess contrition and an undertaking to mend his ways, and an offer to replace the flagstaff himself.

The flagstaff was replaced without his help. Despite his letter to FitzRoy, recalcitrant again, Heke demolished it in January 1845 — twice. The second time was an act of solitary defiance. He left his men below, walked up Maiki

Hill with his axe, brushed aside Waka Nene's Maori guard, and chopped it down. After this third assault, there was respite for a few weeks. Missionary Henry Williams suggested it would be prudent not to replace the flagpole because its presence incited anger among some Maori with its evocation of total British control; but a blockhouse was built and garrisoned around a new flagstaff that was sheathed in iron and set in concrete. For Heke, who knew by this time that Governor FitzRoy had called for military assistance from New South Wales, this was a challenge.

On 11 March, Heke's ally, Te Ruki Kawiti, with about two hundred men, attacked an approach to the town guarded by a detachment of sailors and marines from the British warship, *Hazard*. With the ship's commander, Captain Robertson-Macdonald, in charge, the British fought desperately to hold their position until Robertson-Macdonald was seriously wounded. Meanwhile, on Maiki Hill, most of the garrison troops moved out of the flagstaff blockhouse to watch the action, leaving only four of the twenty soldiers inside. Heke's men entered the briefly undermanned blockhouse, killed those left inside and, after more than an hour of hard work, destroyed the sturdy new flagstaff. The ruse of Kawiti's distraction had worked but, as Heke had more than a hundred warriors with him, the blockhouse would almost certainly have fallen to him anyway.

The battle between the sailors and marines and Kawiti's

men was savage but brief. It's unlikely that the two rebellious chiefs intended to sack the town until Lieutenant Philpotts, who took command after Captain Robertson was wounded, ordered evacuation to the ships in the bay. One reason given later, when Philpotts was criticised for premature evacuation, was that the town's magazine had blown up and left them without ammunition to hold the Maori off, a claim discounted afterwards.

There is even some disagreement about exactly when the magazine exploded and destroyed some nearby cottages. Philpotts was clearly a difficult man given to eruptions of temper. In Auckland before the *Hazard* left for Kororareka, he had fought an inconclusive duel with a newspaper editor he had insulted in a hotel bar. In Kororareka he foolishly abused missionary Henry Williams for corrupting and encouraging Heke. Philpotts proved a brave man at the end, though, killed as he tried to breach the impregnable palisade at Ohaeawai in the face of withering fire from the defenders.

The evacuation from Kororareka meant Maori were able to embark on plunder and arson but without showing any animosity towards the locals, even helping some of them to collect their belongings and escape. Indeed there is an echo of Hongi Hika's reported dying words in Heke's statement at the time: 'To the soldiers only, who are enemies to our power, to our authority over the land, also to our authority over our people, let our hearts be dark.'

By the next day, as the evacuees sailed away, the town was burning. At Heke's insistence, according to the Reverend Robert Burrows, the Anglican and Catholic churches survived along with the headquarters and print shop of the Catholic Bishop Jean Baptiste Pompallier and some nearby cottages. The evacuees headed out of the bay for Auckland aboard the Royal Navy eighteen-gun sloop, *Hazard*, with a usual complement of one hundred and twenty-five; a United States Navy corvette, *St Louis*; an English whaler, *Matilda*; a Government brig, *Victoria*; a schooner, *Dolphin*; and some were aboard *Flying Fish*, Bishop Selwyn's small vessel on which he had sailed from Auckland.

Before departing with its forlorn refugee passengers, the *Hazard*, under Lieutenant Philpotts, bombarded the town. The presence of the *St Louis* demonstrates a continuing interest in the South Pacific by the United States. In fact, there was an undercurrent of opinion that the United States consul and associates had encouraged Maori aggression and that they had even helped arm them.

The many accounts of the events that led to the sacking of Kororareka suggest a remarkable randomness. No one seemed to know what caused the explosion of the magazine, which was inside a stockade owned by Samuel Polack, merchant and brewer. There can be no doubt that Kawiti and Heke intelligently planned and audaciously carried out the diversionary attack and the capture of the blockhouse as a dramatic show of defiance, but it's highly unlikely they had any intention of sacking the town. Following panic among some local residents and Lieutenant Philpotts' perhaps premature decision to flee, events seemed to spin out of anyone's control but complete anarchy did not prevail.

Bishop Selwyn wrote later: 'In the midst of much that was fearful, there was much also that proved the indirect effect of religion and civilisation on the minds of the natives. I may add the following: First the wounded and the women and children were allowed to embark without molestation; then after the explosion of the fortified house [the magazine] the whole force was suffered to retreat on board the ships without a shot being fired; a single soldier who was left behind after the abandonment of the town, was allowed to be carried off by a boat from the ship . . . ' Some Europeans were allowed to return to the town to gather possessions. Ignoring the assumption that Maori had no cultural code of chivalry before 'civilisation' arrived, we can accept that loot and arson may have been on the agenda but not rape and pillage.

Nevertheless, understandably, Aucklanders were disturbed by the news of what had happened after the soldiers arrived — 'disappointed and dejected', according to one report — accompanying a large number of dispirited civilians. Although Heke had shown no interest in interfering with the lives of Northland settlers — and, according to historian James Belich, had never intentionally harmed any civilian — many fled from their settlements to Auckland when they heard about what had happened at Kororareka. Inflamed rumours that Heke was about to march south with a thousand warriors led to military training for the local population and defensive positions being prepared. Property prices dropped as some people abandoned Auckland for Sydney.

Excerpts from the diary of Mr W. T. Bainbridge, a tutor at St John's College in Auckland, give a picture of the kind of panic spreading through the town during the week after the arrival of evacuees before troops arrived from Sydney.

Monday, March 17th: *Reports not to be depended upon still continue to disturb the public, and, amongst the rest, that Heke had arrived off Kaipara on his way to Auckland. It is utterly without foundation.*

In the afternoon I walked into town and saw preparations were commenced for fortifying the church. The barracks are being placed in a state of defence. A trench is being dug and breastwork thrown up. A blockhouse is also in a state of forwardness. It will command the road leading past the back from the church . . .

Tuesday, March 18th: *One of the shopkeepers, with a very long countenance, assured us that it would be very advisable to lay in a quantity of provisions, for all kinds of articles would be, in a week's time, materially raised in price. I suppose it is on account of being 'war-time'.*

The American [the warship St Louis] *sailed this morning on her way, it is reported, to warn the American whalers from the Bay [of Islands], and from thence to Tahiti to send assistance to us.*

Friday, March 21st: *I cannot tell what would be the result if the troops do not arrive very shortly. Many intend to go out of the country, and some may possibly go out of their minds. Inquiries are continually being made, such as 'How far are the Maoris on their way to Auckland?', 'Do you think the fortifications will be sufficiently manned?', 'Is it known whether troops have started from Sydney or not?'. As many as can 'raise the wind' appear to be decided upon the 'necessity of leaving the country'.*

Saturday, March 22nd: *This evening I went aboard the* Slains Castle, *which is crammed with persons terrified at the state of affairs. A man in his eagerness to obtain a passage to Sydney sold his three houses for £15; and another, having a better knowledge of the value of property, sold a very good house for his passage money — namely £10. I should think they were both mad.*

For many Ngapuhi, the abandonment of Kororareka was a disaster. It meant the end of any trade at all through the port, diminished as it had already been by the removal of the capital. The antagonism of many influential northern chiefs hardened towards Heke and Kawiti, which was just as well for FitzRoy and his successor, George Grey, who arrived to take over the governorship towards the end of 1845. United, the northern iwi, which represented about forty per cent of the national Maori population, would have been even more formidable opposition to the military resources available to the governor at that time. As it was, the fight for Kororareka was the only time during the whole of the New Zealand Wars that Maori outnumbered their military opponents.

It was not lost on Governor FitzRoy in Auckland that the sacking of Kororareka was the first co-ordinated, prolonged Maori attack on British authority since the country had become a colony and, with a large force arriving from Sydney, he wasted no time in pursuing the two rebellious chiefs.

After Kororareka, Heke began building a pa at Puketutu, on the shores of Lake Omapere, in his home territory of Kaikohe. He knew that Governor FitzRoy had declared martial law in the Bay of Islands and was assembling a force to pursue and capture him. It was led by Lieutenant-Colonel William Hulme, an experienced officer, and commander of the 96th Regiment of Foot. He left Auckland with about four thousand and sixty men, three hundred of them regulars from the 96th and 58th regiments, supplemented by seamen, marines and local volunteers.

His first mission was to attack the pa at Otuihu of Pomare II on 30 April 1845. Based on misinformation that he was a troublesome ally of Heke's, the pa was razed, its residents dispersed and Pomare himself arrested and taken to Auckland aboard the HMS *North Star*. He was released and given some personal compensation.

After this false start, Hulme and his troops sailed north and landed at Onewhero Bay on 3 May and marched to Puketutu. The pa was incomplete when the British forces arrived four days later. It had defensively solid palisades on three sides but a more penetrable fence at the back, unfinished mainly because of continuing skirmishes with kupapa. They were led by Hokianga chief Tamati Waka Nene, who continued to support the government into the big wars of the 1860s.

Colonel Hulme, a Mancunian by birth and upbringing, was eventually blamed for tactical blunders as the reality of Heke and Kawiti's victory at Puketutu became apparent. Governor FitzRoy somehow quickly turned the defeat — his wish fathering the need — into a victory for public consumption. He claimed at first that Heke and Kawiti had 'fled to the woods . . . beaten and dispersed'. It wasn't long before Hulme was castigated for launching an ill-organised and inadequate operation. A year later, retired from the army after the Ohaeawai defeat, he bought a house in Parnell and was appointed Postmaster-General by Governor George Grey. The house, which became known as Hulme Court, still exists under Historic Places Trust protection.

The British force took four days to march the

24 kilometres from Onewhero Bay to Puketutu and a harsh coming they had of it. They were impeded by continuous cold rain as they trudged over the rough terrain. Archdeacon Robert Burrows had acted as an envoy on behalf of the British in a bid to forestall fighting. Heke was supported by about two hundred men but, although clearly outnumbered, declined to surrender. The British had no artillery but a missile called Constellation rocket, which proved an ineffective weapon. Hulme quickly became aware of the fort's weakness at the rear and launched an attack.

British regular soldiers were, typically, experienced, efficient and disciplined and, during the brutal fight that followed, Heke's men were forced back. They were struggling to hold their ground, when a force led by Kawiti caught the British in a tactical sandwich. Kawiti had arrived the day before with about one hundred and forty warriors and had stayed hidden in the bush until an opportune moment — which came just as the soldiers appeared to be gaining the upper hand against Heke and breaching the pa fence. They were forced to turn to defend their rear and were gaining control over Kawiti's warriors when they were attacked again by Heke's men from within the pa. As they were pushing back into the pa, Kawiti struck a second time. The British had by then lost thirteen men and thirty-nine wounded. Those still fighting were exhausted. Hulme had to pull back.

Maori losses are uncertain but probably about the

same. Kawiti was wounded and one of his sons killed. With one of the chivalrous acts that confused but drew the admiration of his enemy, Heke buried the British dead left on the battlefield, with the help of the Reverend Burrows.

Something Maori took from Puketutu was a determination not to meet British troops in open battle again, especially as they were likely to be outnumbered. The disciplined aggression of the Redcoats made them formidable in the kind of open-field, hand-to-hand fighting at which they were expert and with which they had come close to overcoming Heke and Kawiti. But Puketutu seems, in the context of what followed in Northland and later in Taranaki, to be an example of the British underestimating Maori tactical adroitness.

Kawiti retired to his home area at Waiomio. Heke moved to a small pa of his at Te Ahuahu and it was there that he suffered his most decisive defeat — at the hands of Maori. Waka Nene's kupapa had been at Puketutu but had not taken part in the battle, possibly because Hulme assumed he would not need them. After his move to Te Ahuahu, Heke left the pa inadequately guarded when he went to Okaihau to kill cattle for food. A group of kupapa moved in and took possession. They were quickly joined by Waka Nene's men. Heke marshalled his warriors and attempted to re-take the pa but was soundly defeated by Waka Nene and his allies in a major battle. He was wounded in the encounter. He moved on to Ohaeawai to build a sturdy, defensive pa. Although settlers and the government feared that the success at Kororareka and Puketutu would attract more Maori to his cause, some of Heke's men abandoned him.

On 20 May, the Reverend Burrows found Heke sick with a sore throat, although in no way repentant, according to historian T. L. Buick. After Te Ahuahu, he had had a bullet removed from a thigh wound. At the end of his conversation with Burrows, Heke is reported to have said: 'On what terms do you think the governor would make peace?' Burrows suggested Heke write to FitzRoy. The letter, dated the following day, was delivered to the Governor by Major Cyprian Bridge of the 58th Regiment.

Heke wrote: 'I have no opinion to offer in this affair, because a death's door has been opened. Where is the correctness of the protection offered by the Treaty? Where is the correctness of the goodwill of England? Is it in her great guns? Is it in her Congreve rockets? Is the good will of England shown in the curses of Englishmen and in their adulteries? Is it shown in their calling us slaves? Or is it shown in their regard for our sacred places? . . .

'The Europeans taunt us. They say, "Look at Port Jackson, look at China and all the islands; they are but a precedent for this country. That flag of England which takes your country is the commencement." After this the French, and after them the Americans, told us the same . . . We will die for our country that God has given us . . .

'If you say we are to fight, I am agreeable; if you say you

will make peace with your enemy, I am equally agreeable. I am on my own land . . . '

Major Bridge was reported as saying the Governor found the letter 'not satisfactory' and 'no basis for peace'.

The motive for Waka Nene and his followers to remain an ally of the British was clearly a mixture of belief that supporting them was the best way to enjoy the benefits of the Pakeha presence and also a way of settling old utu scores with the Heke and Kawiti hapu. It was suggested that his special dislike for Heke was because of his deep-dyed hatred for Hongi Hika, Heke's father-in-law.

Troops continued to arrive from Sydney, including Lieutenant-Colonel Henry Despard, a man with experience in India, who was commissioned to assume command of all troops in New Zealand by Sir Maurice O'Connell, commander of forces and Lieutenant-Governor of New South Wales. Despard was by all accounts an irascible, impatient man but he agreed with Hulme's conviction that artillery would be needed to effect entry into a Maori pa. And nothing could have been more obvious than that if a description of the pa, by then under construction at Ohaeawai, is accurate.

It was about 80 metres long and 46 wide. Every wall was broken by an angle or projection so that no part of its length could be approached without the risk of meeting enfilading fire. The outside wall was built of young puriri trees cut from the neighbouring forest. They were sunk almost two metres into the ground and rose three metres above the ground. The poles were bound together with vines and a flax curtain around the base made it bullet-proof. Less than a metre inside the outer wall was a sturdy second wall and, according to Arthur Thomson, MD, surgeon-major in the 58th, there were 'three rows of palisades, the two outer being close together and six feet from the inner fence'.

A zig-zag trench ran around most of the perimeter inside the second wall. It enabled defenders to step up to ledges and fire while being virtually invisible to soldiers on the charge.

Even more important in view of the forthcoming assault from British cannon, Kawiti had, as James Belich put it, 'independently invented the anti-artillery bunker'. The defenders could safely remain in deep pits under wooden beams with earth piled on top.

The Reverend Burrows was watching for a day as they built the pa under the direction of Kawiti, but was then warned politely to go away in case he got to know too much; and Henry Williams was also kept out as he and Burrows tried to urge peace negotiations.

The British force and the guns were landed at Kerikeri and made hard work of the trek through to Waimate with bullock drays and horse-drawn carts to move supplies and the guns — two six-pounders and two twelve-pounders on newly constructed gun carriages. They assembled at the Waimate Mission and arrived at Ohaeawai on 23 June. The barrage began with the cannon moved about to hit the palisades from various positions. A much larger thirty-two-pounder from the *Hazard* was called up later in the week of the siege and joined the artillery assault 90 metres from the palisades but without having much visible effect on the stout fortress.

One day during the week-long siege, according to Arthur Thomson, 'the enemy made a sortie from the pa and attacked Walker's [Nene's] position; and so sudden and unexpected was this sally that a British flag was taken, and Colonel Despard and some senior officers only escaped by a ridiculous and undignified flight. This token of success was hoisted inside the fortification under Heke's flag.' There were other skirmishes but they were risky given the strength of Nene's force.

On 1 July, Despard ordered an assault, pitting two hundred and fifty redcoats against what they thought would be demoralised Maori defenders. They assembled quietly trying for surprise but after they broke into a run and were about 20 metres from the palisades, many were cut down by a deadly musket fusillade. The soldiers nevertheless carried on. They began to tear at the outer fence and pushed at least one assault ladder into place but the intense and accurate fire from within the pa continued until Despard, watching with dismay as his crack troops fell, had the bugler sound the retreat.

William Henry Free, a member of the Light Company of the 58th Regiment that charged the pa that day, told journalist and author James Cowan, many years later: 'I did not see a single Maori all this time — only flashes and smoke, and my comrades falling all around me. The Maories in their sheltered pits just poked the muzzles of their guns under the outer stockade and we could do nothing. The stockade was ten feet high and we were helpless.'

He said an assault ladder was set against the outer palisade but for anyone to try to climb it would have meant certain death. He reckoned that it was no more than seven minutes of carnage between the order to charge and their return to base and yet: 'In our Light Company alone we had twenty-one killed . . . '

The Ohaeawai battle was a debacle for the British. One hundred and ten soldiers killed or wounded — one of the most comprehensive defeats suffered by the British Army in its years of colonial expansion. When the news reached London there was genuine concern whether New Zealand could continue as a British colony in the face of such resistance. Henry Williams also briefly harboured a doubt.

Free claimed: 'Nothing was explained to us before we charged. We just went at the strong stockade front under orders from a Colonel who did not know his business and who had a contempt for Maori.'

By the time Free talked with Cowan, the claim that Despard was rash and incompetent had become inscribed into our national mythology — much as Hulme was blamed for the defeat at Puketutu — perhaps to obscure the fact that Maori, particularly at Ohaeawai, could have out-thought and outfought the disciplined might of the British Empire. It has been reported that senior officers advised Despard against a frontal charge because two apparent breaches in the outer palisade were 'insufficiently broken', and it may be claimed that he was too impatient. But his defenders say his was a reasonable assumption that the defenders would have been decimated and demoralised by the anti-personnel shells poured into the pa for a week before he ordered the charge, and that their morale would have been further shattered by the sight of two hundred and fifty redcoats on the charge. Also in Despard's mind was the certainty that an impasse, with defenders well stocked with food and ammunition, would have been received with irritation and anxiety by Governor FitzRoy and the people of Auckland.

So, by 1 July, Despard and at least some of his fellow officers considered that the anti-personnel shelling into the pa must have caused multiple casualties and have affected the morale of the defenders. Major Bridge wrote a few days before the infantry assault on the pa: 'A constant fire was kept up by the guns of shell, ball and grape till dark. Many hit and burst in the pa and I fancy they must have lost many men.' Two days later he wrote: 'About 2 a.m. two shots of shell were fired into the pa from the hill, which must have astonished the weak minds of the natives.'

Despard had the numbers and neither the soldiers or their leaders had any foreknowledge, or could have been expected to have known, that Kawiti's men had created, behind the outer stockade and in a remarkably short time, a safe and secure set of trenches and bunkers that enabled them to survive and be confidently ready for the fight. Only in recent years since historians, notably James Belich, have gone back through primary sources has the military adaptability of Maori been understood.

Waka Nene and his warriors were present at Ohaeawai and fought Kawiti's men when they emerged on distracting skirmishes during the week-long siege but did not take part in the attack on the pa. Despard didn't feel he needed them and it is doubtful whether Nene thought it prudent to attack the way they did, possibly because he had some knowledge of the arrangements within the stockade.

Did Colonel Despard have contempt for Maori? A story has been told that a few weeks before Ohaeawai, Nene called on Despard to pay his respects and offer his help against Kawiti and Heke and was politely told that when he wanted help from 'savages', he would ask for it. Fortunately — according to Jack Lee in his book *I Have Named It the Bay of Islands* — 'there were no volunteers with the temerity to translate this remark'.

Even earlier, on their way to Puketutu, the British force of about four hundred men under Colonel Hulme were met by Waka Nene who also had about four hundred men. Arthur Thomson reported: 'The soldiers were amazed at the first sight of their friends, and a war dance executed in honour of the English host, with Walker Nene's wife in the front rank marking time, added much to the singularity of the alliance. The soldiers of the 58th Regiment just arrived from England could scarcely believe they were brought to the antipodes to fight in alliance with a rabble of cannibals entirely destitute of that prompt obedience which distinguishes an army from a mob.'

After three weeks of successfully defending their pa at Ohaeawai, Kawiti and Heke abandoned it, giving their enemy the chance to examine the layout inside. The British soldiers and their commanders then realised they had seriously underestimated the resourcefulness of their opponents. According to one report, when Despard inspected the inside of the pa, nothing would convince him that the builders did not have the assistance of some European skilled in the art of fortification. But another officer present is reported to have said: 'I think this will be a lesson to us not to make too light of our enemies . . . '

As James Belich put it: 'The 100 Ngapuhi warriors at Ohaeawai had demonstrated their capacity to resist an Imperial power by defeating the best soldiers in the world, and they knew it.'

Not long after the British retreat, the defenders came out and their haka was a fearful thing to see. Thomson again: 'Never did British troops pass a more dreadful night than the troops before Ohaeawai after this unsuccessful assault. Huddled together in constant expectation of an attack they could not shut their ears to the groans of the dying, the moans of the wounded, and the shrieks of the captured soldier of the 99th Regiment who was tortured every half hour . . . '

At least partly to placate worried settlers and Aucklanders, Governor FitzRoy didn't accept the defeat at first on the grounds that Kawiti and Heke had left the pa and retired to their respective home territories. They were now under some economic pressure as the planting season approached and, anyway, it was Maori practice to abandon a fighting pa in which blood had been spilt.

Five months followed without fighting, a period during which FitzRoy attempted to arrange a peaceful conclusion to the War in the North, using missionaries as emissaries. He insisted on the confiscation of some land, not much of it belonging to either Heke or Kawiti, which made his offer seem like a gesture without much meaning. Heke wavered but stayed loyal to Kawiti who remained firm. He was building an even more extraordinary fort on his land at Ruapekapeka.

More troops were arriving and, in September, FitzRoy was replaced by Captain George Grey, Governor of South Australia, which, incidentally, was the only other colony settled under the idealistic programme devised by Edward Gibbon Wakefield and adopted by the New Zealand Company. Grey was the son of a lieutenant-colonel in the British army who died fighting under the Duke of Wellington against Napolean's army in Spain — not long before Grey was born. He served with the British Army in Ireland for several years and became interested in migration as a solution to over-crowding and poverty. After leading exploration expeditions in Western Australia he was appointed to govern South Australia. His record there impressed London enough to appoint him to the post in troubled New Zealand.

On his arrival, Grey was advised that a peace offer had been made by FitzRoy via the missionaries. He needed to honour that but he put a time limit on a response from Heke and Kawiti. He received none. He immediately became involved in the planning for an immense British attack on the pa at Ruapekapeka, where Kawiti had developed even further the defences against artillery that had served his warriors so well at Ohaeawai. Grey and Colonel Despard had many more troops and resources available than had been employed against the disaffected chiefs at Ohaeawai with such disastrous consequences. This time they knew they had to achieve a victory.

Kawiti had built an extraordinary pa at Ruapekapeka, more robust even than Ohaeawai. 'The Bat's Nest', as it was known, was 155 metres by 65 metres with the stout palisades at angles to allow enfilading fire. It was on a ridge backing on to thick bush.

Arthur Thomson, who joined the 58th Regiment the year following the Ruapekapeka campaign, wrote: 'From an inspection, the troops saw that an assault would have been attended with severe loss, and it was universally admitted that the natives were becoming masters in the science of fortification. Okaihau (Puketutu) was a weak place to an enemy with cannon; Ohaeawai was better adapted for resisting a cannonade; while Ruapekapeka was the strongest of the three, and afforded most shelter to the besieged.'

He explained: 'In an English fort the ditch is deep, and outside the defences; in a New Zealand pa the ditch is shallow and inside the palisades. In an English fort the ditch is made to obstruct the enemy; in a New Zealand pa the ditch is made to cover the defenders, who stand in it and fire at the besiegers.'

Thomson was a remarkable Scot. He graduated with an MD from the University of Edinburgh, and was awarded a gold medal for his thesis on the worldwide influence of climate on health and morbidity. He served with the British Army in India and came to New Zealand to join the 58th. He stayed for eleven years, wrote reports on how healthy the New Zealand climate was, and his remarkable two-volume *The Story of New Zealand: Past and Present – Savage and Civilised* was published in London in 1859, the first written history of the country. He had three children by a Maori partner while living in Auckland and was reported as leaving the country on orders, reluctantly.

It's important to note Kawiti's genius. Lieutenant H. C. Balneavis, who later became Deputy Adjutant-General, Militia and Volunteers, with headquarters in Auckland, wrote in his diary: 'Ruapekapeka was found a most extraordinary place — a model of engineering.' A few ex-British officers were so impressed that two of them made models of the pa for display in London: one at the Great Exhibition in 1851, and the other at the United Service Museum.

The pa was strategically placed, far enough away from where the British troops landed at Kawakawa to make access long and arduous for the men, their supplies and the cannon. But this time the campaign had more naval back-up for the transport of men and supplies and enough troops to protect the overland supply lines (although Kawiti and Heke had not bothered in any of the battles to harass troops and supplies assembling for their assaults). By the end of December 1845, Despard had assembled an army of nearly twelve hundred, including detachments of the 58th and 99th Regiments, sailors, marines and volunteers from Auckland, as well as about four hundred Maori allies under some distinguished leaders, notably Nene again.

It took the army three weeks to slog over the 29 kilometres and assemble in front of Ruapekapeka with their three thirty-two-pounder cannons, an eighteen-pounder, two twelve-pound howitzers and four mortars. The British, who, with their Maori allies, outnumbered the warriors of Kawiti and Heke about three to one, bombarded the pa around the clock for two weeks. It caused few casualties among the defenders but began to damage the outer palisade. Colonel Despard, with Governor Grey at his elbow, still hesitated to launch an assault. He had been moving his fortified camp steadily forward across the area between his base camp and the pa.

Either on the night of 9 January or the next day, Heke arrived from Hikurangi where he had been recovering from his wound. He eluded the vigilance of a Government-friendly hapu chief who had been assigned to keep him pinned down away from Ruapekapeka. He had with him sixty warriors.

The next day, Maori allies, reconnoitring, discovered that the pa seemed to have been abandoned and Waka Nene's men led the way as the attacking force scampered inside. They found Kawiti and a small band of his warriors who fired on the invaders as they retreated. Heavy fighting took place outside the pa as Kawiti's and Heke's men counter-attacked from the bush. The defenders then retreated further into the bush, drawing some British soldiers into ambush. They lost more men than the retreating Maori. However, Despard and, immediately after that, Grey, declared the pa had been assaulted and the enemy beaten and dispersed. For Despard, the claim was for reputation and for Grey for both personal reputation and public relations to placate a nervous colony.

For a hundred and fifty years, the received explanation for the Maori defenders leaving the pa was to attend a Christian service in the bush nearby, assuming the British soldiers would be spending Sunday the same way. Kawiti stayed inside the pa, according to a historian eighty years later, because he was 'an old atheist'. Then, when the body of the defenders realised what had happened they tried to fight their way back into the pa. This view is questionable. Maori had shown no such sensitivity towards fighting on Sundays in the past since their introduction to Christianity.

They may have been driven out for respite from the noise and concussion of what was a massive, unimaginable artillery pounding over two weeks and not expected an attack that day; and then tried to fight their way back into the pa when they realised that the enemy had begun to take possession of it. One British observer suggested that the defenders may have run out of supplies because little or no food was found in the abandoned pa. However, many historians suggest this was unlikely given the fact that access to and from the rear of the pa seemed easy enough.

Given the nature of the fighting in the bush, the explanation offered by James Belich seems the most plausible. Heke had arrived the day before and convinced them it was futile to sit tight in a pa as it was battered by cannon. Belich wrote that, persuaded by Heke, '. . . the idea was that the British would be allowed to occupy Ruapekapeka. Under the impression that they had surprised the garrison they would then pursue the Maoris into the bush, only to be ambushed from prepared positions among the trees. Confirmation that this was the Maori intention was provided by Colonel Despard himself. After the battle Despard examined prepared defences built of tree trunks in the bush behind the pa . . . '

The plan almost worked. Some of the British soldiers did chase Maori into the bush and suffered most of their total of forty-five casualties. In the confusion, Maori also suffered most of their casualties because they did not hold the ambush positions but tried to fight their way back into the pa under the illusion that Kawiti had been captured. And once they realised a trap had been set for them, the British were wary about moving into the bush.

Once the defenders had withdrawn from the pa, the British quickly withdrew to the coast. They felt insecure in the bush and had had enough. That was the end of the Ruapekapeka campaign. Kawiti and Heke went back to their homes after a kind of pointless draw. The two chiefs and their warriors had won two of the battles decisively and at least drawn the third, but the truth was that the War in the North was over. Heke and Kawiti made peace with Waka Nene and his men when they went to a hui at Pomare's pa, accompanied by some of their men, which ended what had partly been a power struggle among Ngapuhi.

Grey accepted the peace after the pretended victory mainly because he wasn't in a position to do otherwise.

The three defensive pa at Puketutu, Ohaeawai and Ruapekapeka were different from the usual hapu pa, which were designed and built to protect their own people and their economic interests so strongly dependent on their land. These forts were adapted from their usual defence structures and built specifically by Kawiti and Heke to fight the British on their own terms. Each pa was an advance on the previous one but, because of the specificity of their purpose, they were easy enough to walk away from when their job was done. Which makes one wonder why the British bothered to muster the huge resources of thousands of men and serious money to attack the pa, which were deliberately built in terrain that was difficult to access. They achieved nothing except for the propaganda that Governor Grey and the military squeezed from the simple misread of the fact that Maori abandoned these fighting pa after inflicting defeat and humiliation on the British in two of the battles and were never defeated in the north.

Better resourced than his predecessor, Grey was an energetic, ambitious, self-promoting politician and for him a lot was at stake: a young man in a new job, having succeeded in the much less challenging role of Governor of South Australia. FitzRoy had talked of land confiscation as punishment. Grey, wisely, erased that from the agenda, for the meantime anyway. He travelled from Auckland to Kororareka in late November aboard the East Indian-built sloop, *Elphinstone*, and inspected the troops gathered there. He joined Despard as the battle for Ruapekapeka progressed and appears even to have taken charge. He desperately needed this army to win and quickly claimed they had.

While the Establishment was proclaiming 'victories', Heke was free to live as he always had in Northland with more mana than previously. His fight had not been with the European settlers but with the government and the soldiers who, he considered, had taken away his rangatiratanga. He retired to Kaikohe, shrewd enough to know that he would ultimately be swamped by the British and their Ngapuhi, if he didn't accept peace. Also, the battles had had serious economic implications for the Maori involved in the war. Their resources were seriously limited when compared with the men and money available to the Pakeha authorities. And Heke was suffering from tuberculosis, which killed him four years later, in 1850.

The question hung in the air: why did the British pursue a war so costly and yet so unrewarding, especially the last major marshalling of resources for the campaign against Kawiti at Ruapekapeka? James Belich, in his seminal *The New Zealand Land Wars and the Victorian Interpretation of Racial Conflict*, quotes Captain Thomas Collinson on Ruapekapeka: '1100 men were occupied a full month in advancing 15 miles and in getting possession of a pah from which the enemy escaped at the last moment, and escaped with the satisfaction to him of a drawn battle. The question is, was it worthwhile to go through all that laborious march to obtain such a result?'

The real reason was probably that Grey and most Pakeha settlers were fearful that Heke and Kawiti had the capacity to continually create problems and their suppression would send a message to any other Maori considering what the British now regarded as 'rebellion', despite the Treaty provisions as Maori saw them. Also, it would help convince the government in London that New Zealand was a viable colony and placate the rapidly growing number of British settlers that the Pakeha authorities were in control and the 'savages' were not. No doubt the prestige and power of the Empire unconsciously prompted their need for ruthless, punitive suppression of the indigenous people, something they had achieved everywhere else during the expansion in the eighteenth and nineteenth centuries.

Although the defeats by Maori were so often blamed on the incompetence of British commanders, Queen Victoria — 'while lamenting the effusion of blood', as Major Thomson put it — rewarded many of the officers with honours. Colonel Despard became a Commander of the Military Order of the Bath.

However, though the War in the North was over, struggles between Maori and Pakeha more directly over land were not. There was worse to come.

Chapter 4
War in Taranaki

The first Taranaki War seems to have been inevitable looking back from this distance. The growing invasion of Pakeha migrants, as Maori numbers dwindled, didn't consider the Treaty of Waitangi did anything but turn New Zealand into yet another British colony — if they considered it at all.

Maori land that wasn't being cleared of bush for English-style pastoral farming or intensive cropping was seen as 'wasteland' to settlers and there for the taking.

It came down to this. The settlers at New Plymouth, who began arriving in the early 1840s, wanted to buy more land, and they especially coveted the Waitara block. The Te Atiawa who lived there allocated ancestral land to various families to use as their own, as other iwi did in their regions. But tribal law, traditional although unwritten, gave them no right to sell it without the agreement of the iwi through the senior chief. Tribal land, in short, was essentially owned by the iwi.

In 1859, one Te Atiawa leader, Te Teira Manuka,

offered to sell two hundred and forty hectares of land he occupied on the Waitara block — to the government, as mandated by the Treaty. But for the government to accept this, it would have to accept that any Maori allocated land for occupation within tribal boundaries essentially had title to it — as an individual owner in Britain would have — and therefore the right to sell. What was happening, and not only in Taranaki, was that the settlers wanted to smother Maori custom with British law.

Te Teira was in a feud with the senior Te Atiawa chief Te Rangitake Wiremu Kingi, who, with hundreds of his followers, was also living and cultivating on the Waitara block at the time. He insisted that he had the right to veto such a sale on behalf of the iwi as their senior chief. At a meeting with Te Atiawa in Taranaki in March 1859, the Governor, Lieutenant-Colonel Thomas Gore Browne, said he would buy no man's land with disputed title — but then accepted Te Teira's offer.

Wiremu Kingi was reported as saying: 'Listen Governor. Notwithstanding Teira's offer, I will not permit the sale of Waitara to the Pakeha. Waitara is in my hands. I will not give it up. I will not. I will not. I will not.' He then stormed out of the meeting with what Gore Browne felt was a kind of lese-majesty.

Europeans had come late to Taranaki. James Cook anchored off New Plymouth's Ngamotu Beach but high surf, driven onto the coast by the prevailing westerly wind, and the lack of any sheltered anchorage close to the shore, kept him from landing. These rough seas pounding the shore meant it wasn't until the late 1820s that Taranaki Maori had any sustained contact with Europeans. The lack of a natural port dismayed the early European settlers, authorised, they thought, to occupy the land by questionable New Zealand Company purchases. What struck all the earliest arrivals most was the black iron sand along the coast: 'wealth spread out as a carpet', one man wrote to his English family. But, more importantly to them, they saw a place with lots of warm rain with potential for farming of the sort they planned.

Wiremu Kingi was born Te Rangitake, but took the name (William King) when he was baptised about 1840. He wasn't the only Maori chief to assume that name during the early years of the eighteenth century but became the most prominent in his time. (William IV was the English King until 1837, immediately before Victoria became Queen.) At the end of the 1840s, several hundred Te Atiawa returned to the iwi's ancestral land and resettled on the southern bank of the Waitara River. They had lived for some years at Waikanae, seeking refuge there in the turbulent years during and following the Musket Wars and, for most of them, just in time to escape the powerful marauding Waikato.

Kingi, at least in his sixties, was a respected chief, an imposing man, once described by Archbishop Charles Abraham of Auckland as having 'a fine handsome face, and iron-grey hair, and his giant form of six feet three inches, with breadth in proportion, certainly gave one the idea of a warrior chieftain'. A picture from the time shows high cheekbones and a moko that gave his face a determined forward thrust. From the 1840s, the incessant demand for more land from all the New Zealand Company settlers built up pressure on the government to force sales from Taranaki Maori. In the mid-1850s, Kingi supported the Puketapu people in northern Taranaki, who refused to sell land despite pressure from a faction within the hapu. Then he sought peace within the region by trying to stand aloof from criticism as the New Plymouth settlers began to regard him as the major obstacle to expansion. He was vilified in their newspapers.

Governor Gore Browne, a man with a luxuriantly whiskered face even for those times, joined the army in 1824 at the age of seventeen and commanded a Welsh regiment during the disastrous British campaign in Afghanistan between 1839 and 1842. He was, for four years before his appointment to New Zealand, Governor of St Helena, a tiny island in the South Atlantic. He served in New Zealand from 1855 until 1861, a term between the two gsovernorships of George Grey (buffered at each end by Robert Wynyard's service as Government Administrator and Acting Governor).

Gore Browne's initial preoccupation was to set up a structure for self-government for the colony, which was granted by the Colonial Office from 1852, except that the Governor retained Maori affairs and commanded the only armed force. Despite genuine and well-meaning attempts to progress Maori interests, the governor persisted that Te Teira had the right to sell and Kingi no right to veto a sale.

However, he should not historically shoulder the full blame for the intransigence of his position. He was supported by the Colonial Office and by substantial majorities in the Pakeha-controlled General Assembly. The settlers not only wanted Waitara badly but sensed that if individual Maori were legally able to sell bits of tribal land, more of it would become more readily available.

Browne's decision was to cost hundreds of lives. With pressure from settlers to buy more and more land and the determination of Maori not to yield, war soon became inevitable and both sides began to prepare for it.

New Plymouth was a kind of kitset settlement with people and their belongings moved more or less as a body from England, originally organised by the Plymouth Company, which was subsumed in 1841 by the New Zealand Company. The settlement suffered greatly from the lack of a harbour, so important for transport in a country with a crumpled hinterland that made land transport difficult, although reasonable land access to Wellington was available and it wasn't a long sail for small coastal vessels that could manage the bar over the Waitara river mouth in fine weather.

The Richmond and Atkinson families, closely related by marriage, the Hursthouses, Messengers and the Kings, and other Taranaki settlers — mostly from

Devon, Cornwall and other southern England counties — relished a foothold in their new country.

Harry Atkinson, a future Premier, who pit-sawed timber for his first house, later returned to New Plymouth from a visit to England to say he was proud to be English but, nevertheless, New Zealand was his home. He was, indeed, at home in Taranaki and, along with many of his fellow settlers, knew the land and the bush so well he proved an adept and courageous bush fighter when war broke out. The later careers of the families of the Kings, Atkinsons and Richmonds lent Taranaki a good deal of influence on the national stage, the Atkinsons and Richmonds in politics and the Kings in commerce and health services.

Anyone who made the decision to spend up to five months in a sailing ship to come to New Zealand was either a determined, tough and hopeful person or a reject from Britain. Harry Atkinson certainly had those positive qualities but personifies the predominant attitude of so many settlers. He vigorously backed military settlements in Taranaki at the expense of Maori interests and unquestionably believed in the natural superiority of what he would have called Anglo-Saxon civic culture.

Atkinson still held these views in his later life on the national stage when his social and political attitude was, for his time, powerfully liberal. Much the same could be said of John Ballance, from Whanganui, later the first Liberal Party Premier. But, even more immoderate,

New Plymouth's Charles W. Richmond, who once referred to Maori as 'contumacious savages', campaigned indefatigably and vociferously to legalise individual titles for their land so it could be more easily bought by settlers.

So Atkinson and the other Taranaki settlers saw their role as bringing British government culture, with its traditional law and order, to this country, gradually subsuming Maori into civilised compliance. There is no reason to believe that they were not sincere in their belief of British superiority. In the case of the Waitara block they coveted, this sincerity was backed by the pragmatic desire for its agricultural potential and prospects for a small ships' port. A surveyor, Frederic Carrington (who later became Taranaki's Provincial Superintendent), chose the site and planned the town of New Plymouth in 1841. He had considered the banks of the Waitara River but instead chose the site 10 miles to the south, near New Plymouth's signature Sugar Loaves.

What was certain even then was that anywhere on the west coast of the country was going to be problematic for shipping. The river entrance — because of the littoral drift that shifts sand bars down the west coast of both islands — would have been as unsatisfactory as any of the country's other west coast river-mouth ports have proved to be, but would have been a haven for small craft. There is no doubt, though, that Carrington and his fellow settlers were impressed with the potential for Waitara, the area that became the crucible in which the first Taranaki

War was fought at the beginning of the 1860s.

Chief Justice Sir William Martin, making a case for the Te Atiawa claim to preserve their ownership of the Waitara block, quoted from a letter Carrington wrote in 1841: 'If we are deprived of this river [the Waitara], we lose the only harbour we have for small craft and also the most valuable district for agriculture; in lieu of which we shall have a dense forest which will require much capital, time and labour to clear.' What they were disinclined to factor in was that Maori also had a traditional culture with its unwritten but, by them, understood code of law and custom — and they were in situ. Kingi's case could be made within a framework of fairness and respect for the Treaty, and it was reinforced by a number of independent Pakeha, most notably Sir William Martin, and also the Archdeacon of Kapiti, the Reverend Octavius Hadfield, and Bishop George Selwyn.

In 1860 (the war had started earlier that year), Sir William wrote a book, *The Taranaki Question*, 'for circulation among members of the Imperial Parliament and Members of the General Assembly of New Zealand'. It was a detailed, trenchant, but also measured defence of the iwi's right to the land at Waitara and Wiremu Kingi's right to veto the attempted sale by Te Teira. Hadfield was a persistent defender of Wiremu Kingi and his right to deny the Governor's insistent demand that Te Teira's piece of land should be available for sale. In 1860, he wrote a letter to the Duke of Newcastle, Secretary of State for the Colonies, which opened with: 'When a flagrant act of injustice has been committed by the Governor of a British colony in the name of Her Majesty the Queen, it is not easy to determine what course to pursue. If, indeed, an Englishman were the sufferer, either the Courts of law or the public press would afford a sufficient guarantee that the injustice would be remedied. But when an aboriginal chief is affected by such an act of injustice, neither of these avail to him . . . '

It is a long and indignant letter in which he says he had known Wiremu Kingi for twenty years and in which he asks: 'Are chiefs to be debarred from all right to defend their titles in a competent court of law?' He claims: 'Not long since, a girl, who was affianced to Teira's brother, preferred William King's son and married him. It is well known here that Teira immediately meditated revenge for this slight put upon his brother.'

Over the following two years, and well after the fighting was under way, Hadfield indefatigably sent increasingly angry letters and newspaper articles to London, rebutting 'the Governor's calumnious imputations against me', and charging him with causing the Taranaki War, 'the real object [of which] was nothing else than the acquisition of 600 acres of land which the settlers were anxious to obtain, and which the Governor thought were "essential for the consolidation of the Province"'.

Gore Browne had moral support, though, from most European settlers nationally, and the New

Plymouth settlers were wholly committed to expansion. On 20 February 1860, a survey party led by chief surveyor Octavius Carrington and accompanied by his assistant Charles Hursthouse was obstructed by Maori as it prepared to work on the Waitara block. After the surveyors returned to New Plymouth, Wiremu Kingi was warned to apologise and withdraw his opposition within twenty-four hours. He replied that he loved white people very much, that he did not want war but he would keep the land.

The officer in charge of the military contingent at New Plymouth, Lieutenant-Colonel Murray, proclaimed martial law on 22 February. The Taranaki Militia and the Taranaki Rifle Volunteer Company were called to active service and armed as many of the outer settlers abandoned their homes and migrated to the town. A few stayed on their farms and some of them paid the price as Te Atiawa, with support from south Taranaki's Ngati Ruanui, plundered and burnt houses and killed occupants who had not fled into New Plymouth.

This first Taranaki War lasted for thirteen months, although Maori were far from defeated when a truce was called and sporadic skirmishing continued for some time. It lasted a lot longer than the British or the settlers expected, given the forces and resources available to them and their determination to secure a quick and convincing victory. There were other battles in the province over coming years but this first Taranaki War was the one that set a course for the government to arbitrarily decide who would own land in the province. It was the beginning of more than a decade of large-scale strife between Pakeha and Maori.

The battles were fought mostly on the accessible land on the coastal strip because that was the land specifically at stake; so there was no point in Maori building pa in the densely bushed and broken terrain on the eastern side of the province — as they had in the Northern War. Wiremu Kingi's warriors were reinforced immediately by other iwi from around the province and later, from time to time, by factions from almost every iwi in the Waikato, including Ngati Maniapoto; but the leaders of Waikato's King movement were reluctant to give strong and official support. It was significant that fewer kupapa chose to support the government in Taranaki as they had in the Northern War (and would do so in the Waikato where the issues were more complex). During the length of the first Taranaki War, the settlers were unable to gain and hold any land any distance from the town as Maori fought a roving defensive war that denied the British the decisive victory that they so badly wanted.

The population of New Plymouth was about two thousand five hundred at the start of the war and journalist and historian James Cowan, in his 1922 *The New Zealand Wars*, estimated that five or six hundred were men between sixteen and fifty-five and thus eligible for service. But the garrison quickly swelled to twice that number with the arrival of regular soldiers from the 56th Regiment. The town then drew back inside tightened boundaries ready for a siege. A stockade was built on a commanding hill and a series of blockhouses were constructed at strategic points nearby.

Most women and children were evacuated to Nelson but the density of the population within the town's constricted area led to health problems as the war drew on. Gore Browne arrived from Auckland on 1 March 1860, accompanied by Colonel Charles Gold of the 65th who took command of the military operation until Major-General Thomas Pratt arrived from Melbourne. Pratt was the officer commanding troops in the Australian colonies and New Zealand.

More regulars arrived with Gore Browne and Gold and from then on Te Atiawa and their allies were outnumbered, often by more than two to one in almost all encounters from the earliest days of the war. As Cowan put it: 'They [Maori] did not at any time outnumber or even equal the whites under arms, but man for man they were better campaigners so long as they were able to choose the land for battle.'

The HMS *Niger*, a barque under the command of Captain Peter Cracroft, arrived the same day as the Governor. She carried twelve thirty-two-pounder guns. Fifty sailors and marines built an entrenchment on a hill on the town's eastern border and mounted a twelve-pounder field piece. Two other ships, the *Cordelia* and the *Pelorous*, described as 'steam corvettes', were sent to support the beleaguered town. Cowan again: '. . . the hundred-strong Taranaki Rifle Volunteer Company, formed in 1858, was the first British volunteer corps to engage an enemy in the field' (in the early battle of Waireka). When the war started, the group was divided into two companies, one led by later New Zealand Premier Captain Harry Atkinson.

In early March 1860, four hundred men under the command of Colonel Gold marched onto the disputed land near the mouth of the Waitara River and began building a substantial redoubt that they used as a base throughout the war. Kingi's men built a pa on the edge of the disputed Waitara block. Named Te Kohia, it became known as the L-pa because of its shape. It had, typically, the double palisades, rifle pits and bunkers. Gold moved against the pa with three companies of the 65th Regiment, some sailors from HMS *Niger* and twenty local cavalry volunteers, one of whom was killed rashly riding in close to carry off the Maori war flag. The pa was battered by artillery and, the next morning, the troops were ready to charge when it was found to be abandoned. Maori casualties are unknown. The first head-to-head engagement of the Taranaki War ended without serious consequences to either side.

On 28 March, about three hundred and fifty soldiers, under the command of Lieutenant-Colonel Murray, set out from New Plymouth to attack a stockade that a report said Maori had set up on the road south to Omata, a few kilometres south-west of New Plymouth, where two farmers and a New Plymouth merchant had been killed in an ambush.

About the same time as the soldiers moved out of the town, a hundred and sixty militia volunteers marched south along the coast to bring in any out-settlers cut off from the town and, if necessary, to outflank any Maori under attack by the main force. The situation became confused as warriors, mainly from Ngati Ruanui, attacked the militia near the beach. The volunteers held out against the attackers but ran short of ammunition. They were also burdened, they claimed, by a number of wounded and, therefore, unable to retreat to the town; so they established a defensive position around a farmhouse. Lieutenant-Colonel Murray is said to have made some attempt to get to the beleaguered militia but then marched back to the town in accordance with Colonel Gold's order to be back by nightfall. They passed a group of fifty or sixty bluejackets from the *Niger* who were resolved to attack the Maori position they had been told was on the road to Omata.

The subsequent battle of Waireka was a brilliant victory — or not, depending on who got to tell the story. For the British, and particularly for the Royal Navy, it was a victory so complete that the death toll of the enemy would have damaged Maori resistance in the south of the province. It was gained, so the story went, by the brazen courage of the bluejackets, led by Captain Cracroft, attacking the pa, climbing into it by leap-frogging one on top of the other while evading Maori musket fire, and killing all the defenders. One claim was that one hundred and fifty Maori were killed.

James Cowan was nothing if not a good reporter and his history of the wars was heavy with first-hand accounts from both sides and he was a fact-conscious writer who did, however, occasionally hitch his style to the melodramatic tales of British Empire glory. He drifted into melodrama, retelling the story of Waireka in 'Boys' Own' language: 'The bluejackets did their work in the traditional naval manner, mostly with the cutlass. Charging up the hill and making little account of the fire from the rifle-pits, they dashed up the stockade with a tremendous cheer.

'Three flags bearing Maori war devices were seen waving above the smoke-hazed palisades. "Ten pounds to the man who pulls down the flags!" shouted Cracroft. Yelling, shooting and slashing, the navy lads were over the stockade in a few moments, "like a pack of schoolboys" in the phrase of a survivor of Waireka. The first man in was [coxswain] William Odgers . . .' Odgers was awarded the Victoria Cross for his exploit, and it was claimed by the military that the comprehensive victory saved the volunteers who were desperately defending their barricaded farmhouse position.

What is clear is that Waireka was not a well-made defensive structure the Maori were so adept at building.

Even at the time there were questions asked about whether there were many Maori in the pa, let alone dozens killed. It is difficult now from whatever evidence exists even to roughly estimate Maori casualties, with figures ranging wildly from one to a hundred and fifty. Given the number of Maori in the war parties at the time, a death toll of the highest claimed by some Pakeha — and only some — would have defined the course of the war over the following few weeks. Waireka seems to have been what historian James Belich described as 'a paper victory', the capture of a pa from a small group of Maori left behind when the main war party abandoned it.

The day after the battle, the *Niger*, flying three captured Maori flags from her mainmast, anchored offshore from a large Maori pa down the coast from New Plymouth and opened fire with shells and rockets but the range was too great for any damage to the pa. Several hundred men from the 13th and 40th Regiments and a unit of the Royal Artillery arrived at New Plymouth during April 1860, and British units under the direction of Colonel Gold spent some weeks marauding — destroying undefended pa and flour mills, burning Maori food stores and removing cattle and horses. Maori retaliated by raiding and burning farm settlements outside New Plymouth.

The first major set-piece battle was at Puketakauere pa, near the mouth of the Waitara River, where Maori built two strongly fortified pa (Puketakauere and Onukukaitara) close together, less than two kilometres from the main British stockade and on higher ground. Te Atiawa warriors were helped by a substantial reinforcing war party from Ngati Maniapoto. Major Thomas Nelson of the 40th Regiment, a veteran of war in Afghanistan and India, was instructed to attack the pa in what Governor Browne and Colonel Gold hoped would be a coup de grace for what they regarded as rebellion. Nelson had three hundred and fifty men, backed by two howitzers, probably less of an advantage in numbers than they had previously enjoyed.

The British force was divided to make a three-pronged attack with about sixty bluejackets and marines in the frontal storming party. They moved out at dawn on 27 June. Many of the Te Atiawa and Ngati Maniapoto warriors, under the direction of Te Atiawa fighting chief, Hapurona, had left the pa and were hiding in the tall fern and waiting in trenches they had prepared in advance in the swampy land. All three attacking groups came under fire from unanticipated directions. As the British regulars began to retreat — steady and organised under the withering fire from the trenches — the warriors leapt from their cover and attacked some of them with tomahawks. That forced a more disorderly withdrawal. British losses were more than thirty killed and as many wounded. Maori losses were considerably less. It was the most decisive victory by Maori in the first Taranaki War and guaranteed that it would be prolonged for months to come.

The victory emboldened the region's iwi and enhanced the sense of insecurity among the settlers, pinned down as they were within New Plymouth's fortified boundaries. Skirmishes close to the town made the inhabitants fearful of a major assault. It also exacerbated division between the settlers and their volunteers and the British regulars, whose commanders were blamed for tactical folly at Puketakauere, as commanders almost always were in the New Zealand Wars when they suffered defeat by Maori. A week later, Major-General Pratt arrived to take direct personal command of the British forces in the province.

The warriors from the Waikato were greatly heartened by the striking victory and when the Maori king, Potatau, died immediately afterwards some restraint was removed from Waikato warriors who went to Taranaki in search of mana and loot as well as the sense that land was an issue worth fighting for. With more hubris than planning, they gathered at Mahoetahi, an old pa site close to the British base at Waitara — a challenge quickly taken up because the pa was inadequately fortified.

The British moved to the attack on 6 November, almost seven hundred of them, mostly army regulars supported by more than a hundred Taranaki volunteers and a small group of kupapa. The estimated Maori strength was about a hundred and fifty, mostly Ngati Haua from the Waikato. The defences at the pa were incomplete and, after British artillery had breached palisades, the regulars launched a formidable, disciplined bayonet charge. They drove the defenders into a swamp and cut them down as they retreated. At least fifty Maori were killed and Cowan estimated that possibly as many were wounded. The defeat was overwhelming.

By December 1860, the likelihood of an immediate Maori attack on New Plymouth was fading and the inevitability of the British eventually wearing down the Maori resistance seemed clear given their numerical advantage and superior armaments and other resources. Also, the regulars were now fighting under the patient, pragmatic leadership of General Pratt. After Mahoetahi, some British troops were removed to protect Auckland as relations between Waikato and the Government deteriorated. But Waikato warriors were still arriving in Taranaki to boost Te Atiawa numbers and some British reinforcements also continued to arrive by sea. Maori built formidable defensive structures on an elevated plateau above the southern bank of the Waitara.

This pa was designed to bar the way inland and was thus dubbed Te Arei, 'The Barrier'. It had formidable palisades, bunkers and rifle pits. Over several weeks there were a number of attacks and counter-attacks as the two armies continually fought for control. General Pratt approached this defensive structure at Te Arei, even more methodically than he had at Mahoetahi. He pushed a long trench/tunnel, or sap — in places two parallel saps — toward the palisades as his heavy artillery, brought in from Auckland, pounded the Maori positions.

The defenders abandoned two subsidiary pa as saps approached. But the engineers then turned their attention to the major Te Arei defensive position. One report was that the main sap extended for a kilometre, with heavily manned redoubts constructed along the way to give some protection to the British as they moved the sap forward towards the pa's defensive structure. The slow, digging advance continued even as the British had to fight off marauding bands of Tainui and Te Atiawa harassing the diggers and filling in sections of the saps. They were still a long way short of the palisades when the campaign ended. A truce was called for three days from 12 March 1861, with Wiremu Tamihana Tarapipipi Te Waharoa, the astute 'Kingmaker' from Ngati Haua, arriving from Waikato to negotiate a peace. Ngati Haua had been deeply involved in the Taranaki fighting and had suffered losses. Fighting was resumed on 15 March but four days later peace resumed after George Grey, who had arrived to begin his second term as Governor at the end of December, called for an inquiry into the cause of the war.

The truce wrought by Wiremu Tamihana was temporary and by no means the end of conflict in Taranaki but when the cost was counted of this first, longest and most destructive of the wars in the province it was clear the settlers would take a long time to re-establish themselves. They more or less had to start over again twenty years after their arrival.

Those of New Plymouth's population who had endured

the siege had been damaged by elevated rates of sickness and death during the siege. Those who were evacuated to Nelson and Wellington began to trickle back, despite the continuing skirmishes. Families such as the Kings built their homes in the town. Their house in the country had been looted and destroyed.

The homes and holdings of one hundred and eighty-seven farming families had been sacked and burnt and one estimate was that the loss of buildings and stock amounted to £200,000 — millions in today's money. They were granted only a tenth of that sum as compensation by the Government. Maori property loss was immediately superficially less but overall they lost almost everything. Wiremu Kingi went to live with Ngati Maniapoto and the Waikato fighters returned to their homes.

The terms agreed that the survey of the Waitara block should be undertaken, that plunder taken from the settlers be returned (it never was), and that Te Atiawa accept not only the 'sovereignty' as spelled out in the Treaty but the full authority of Queen Victoria. Most Taranaki iwi signed the peace agreement, but Ngati Ruanui refused.

Grey was knowledgeable on Maori lore and, after he arrived back in New Zealand for his second term, ruled in May 1863 that the Crown had acted unfairly over the Waitara block and the decision against Wiremu Kingi should be reversed. The prospects for peace may briefly have looked bright, but unfortunately, before Ngati Ruanui knew of this Waitara decision, Grey had ordered the reoccupation of a block at Tataraimaka, 25 kilometres south-west of New Plymouth.

Ngati Ruanui attempted to seal off the land from the British and killed nine of a party of redcoats in an ambush as they moved towards Tataraimaka. This swift and brutal attack aroused violent opposition among the settlers and among the British soldiers now under the command of the immensely experienced Lieutenant-General Sir Duncan Cameron. He replaced Pratt who had returned to Victoria.

As Maori prepared a defensive pa on the Tataraimaka block, Cameron attacked and at least twenty Maori were killed. The truce was dead and any chance of a lasting peace settling over Taranaki for most of the next decade died with it. The major enemy of the settlers this time was not Te Atiawa but Ngati Ruanui with assistance from other south Taranaki iwi and allies from Whanganui.

When Grey arrived for his second term, he was instructed by the Colonial Office to stop Maori moves towards political independence by peaceful means if possible or by military action if not. His plan involved the setting up of local and district councils (runanga) in which chiefs in association with European magistrates would have some say in local government. But the scheme also envisaged European settlement within Maori districts and, more problematic for Maori, a break down from tribal land ownership to individual titles.

The runanga scheme was approved by Premier William Fox, a deep-dyed racist, but Grey discovered a deepened

Maori distrust of Pakeha since his period away from New Zealand. In Taranaki, Maori felt embattled by a catch-22 — the more they attempted to defend their land, the more it was taken as a punishment. In the end, they lost six hundred thousand hectares to Government confiscation.

In August 1865, the Irish-born Major-General Trevor Chute replaced Cameron as commander of British troops in New Zealand. After unrest continued in the province, the decision was taken to subdue with a massive display of force what were seen as intermittent and disheartening outbreaks of rebellion.

Chute, fresh from his role in supporting the ruthless suppression of Indians in the aftermath of the Indian mutiny, had an army of six hundred and twenty men. They left Whanganui in the last days of 1866. This substantial force included infantry, an artillery detachment, the Forest Rangers (a New Zealand militia), and about two hundred and seventy Maori allies. In a scorched earth campaign over six weeks, Chute's men indiscriminately attacked and destroyed fortified pa and peaceful villages, which were the economic underpinning of Maori existence. They took few prisoners.

It was swift, brutal and highly destructive. Nowhere did he meet consolidated or organised resistance as he steamrolled across the province and when the troops arrived back in New Plymouth they were welcomed as heroes. Governor Grey said Chute had shown all the qualities of a great general. Fighting didn't finish in

Taranaki even after the brilliant campaign by Titokowaru who, towards the end of the decade, gained control of southern Taranaki and terrified the local European population and the colonial government. (See Chapter 8: The Throes of Two Great Warriors.)

After his land had been confiscated, Wiremu Kingi moved first to the King Country with Rewi Maniapoto and then to the steep, heavily bushed country in Taranaki, between the upper reaches of the Waitara and Whanganui rivers. It wasn't until early 1872 that Kingi and his followers moved down to their home near Waitara. On 22 February, the twelfth anniversary of martial law in 1860, according to reports in the *Taranaki Herald* at the time, Kingi walked into New Plymouth town, surrounded by about a hundred and fifty of his men, followed by their women and then about two hundred Waikato Maori. He was a tall, now elderly, man. He walked with eyes cast down, never looking at the people lining the footpath to see him. He was dressed in native costume and wore a black skull cap from beneath which his locks of grey hair were visible.

The Pakeha who greeted him included the Native Minister, Donald McLean. It was a time of reconciliation. Wiremu Kingi was on his way to Parihaka to listen to one of the monthly speeches by Te Whiti and Tohu. As Keith Sinclair put it: 'They preached peace but, like many other Maori, had not given in.'

Chapter 5
The Maori King Movement

The symbol of Maori unity under an evolving King movement in the central North Island in the 1850s was worrying to Pakeha authorities in Auckland, many of whom presumed that in Maori minds their monarch would assume status over Queen Victoria.

Pakeha, fearfully, didn't seem to understand how fragile unity was between iwi and even between hapu. They saw only the threat of a large, purposeful Maori army moving north to threaten their existence.

Governor Gore Browne had decided that war against the movement was likely and was preparing for an invasion of the Waikato towards the end of his term in office. His successor at the end of 1861, George Grey, once he had investigated the possibility of placating the King movement, moved quickly to end what he saw as a challenge to the sovereignty of Queen Victoria.

Back in 1835, a Declaration of Independence, appointing a Confederation of United Tribes to establish a country ruled by a tribunal of iwi leaders, was written by the British Government's New Zealand Resident, James Busby, with a little help from his friends: the missionaries Henry Williams and William Colenso. The declaration was constructed around a myth that — because they spoke the same language and had similar cultural traditions — Maori were a nationally conjoined people, saw themselves as one people, one entity, just as the English did in England. Maori were given a flag, then a necessary accoutrement for any country's ships entering a foreign port, but they had nothing to do with the idea of a confederation nor did they have anything to do with its preparation.

Maori, who knew all about where power comes from, regarded Busby as irrelevant, dubbed him a 'man o' war without guns'. In their real world, before European rediscovery, Polynesia had been an isolated culture for at least two thousand years and Maori had been entirely on their own for about five hundred. Iwi would have seen themselves as nations in a separate world — much as, as examples, Germany, France and Russia did — when along came the Dutch, very briefly, and then British, representatives of a united nation ruled by a king (George III, followed by William IV and, in 1837, Queen Victoria). Because they were their whole world, they had no name for themselves as a race until after the European arrival when they called themselves 'Maori', meaning 'normal'.

Nevertheless, in 1835, thirty-four northern chiefs signed the document, which declared New Zealand an independent state and that a council of chiefs, would hold a meeting, a 'hui', each year to make and administer laws. They called upon King William to become their 'parent' and 'protector' and their new status was acknowledged by the British Government, as was their flag.

The political motivation of the British for the attempt to set up this independent nation involved the anarchic presence of many whalers, sealers and traders in the Bay of Islands; the presence of an eccentric, bogus baron, Charles de Thierry, who bought some land on the Hokianga and declared himself king; and the possibility that France or the United States might decide to assume colonial control over the country. France was the other dominant power in the Pacific in the eighteenth and early nineteenth centuries. Whalers from the east coast of the United States were already so common that their currency was acceptable in the Bay of Islands and there was a United States Consul in Kororareka. United States warships were occasional visitors.

Perhaps Maori motivation sprang from a certain war weariness among North Island iwi in the wake of the savage Musket Wars of the 1820s and 1830s. But at the time practical unity was impossible. It wasn't until the 1850s that Maori — realising they were already outnumbered by European immigrants (confirmed by an admittedly sketchy census in 1858), and losing land and political control over their own destiny — began to consider that unity under a king in the manner of the British was a defensive option.

The champion of the movement was Wiremu Tamihana, known by contemporary Pakeha and by historians since as 'the Kingmaker'. By the late 1850s, Tamihana thought the establishment of a single Maori leader, a king, was a way to replace fraying iwi chieftainship with coherent leadership. Born early in the nineteenth century, Tarapipipi was the son of a powerful Ngati Haua chief, Te Waharoa. When he was about thirty and, after he had assumed leadership of Ngati Haua on the death of his father, he came under the influence of the Reverend Alfred Brown at the Anglican-dominated Church Missionary Society at Matamata.

He learnt to read and write, was baptised as Wiremu Tamihana (William Thompson) five years later, and became an influential spiritual leader and teacher. He had taken part in inter-tribal warfare as a young man but after his Christian conversion refused to do so and, instead, began to work for peaceful negotiations. Tamihana was clearly a striking presence. John Gorst lived among Maori in the Waikato for several years in the early 1860s and, later, after an influential career in British politics, wrote: 'I have met many statesmen in the course of my life, but none superior in intellect and character to this Maori chief [Tamihana] whom most people would look upon as a savage.'

The 1852 Constitution Act provided for a council of chiefs representing the regions to work with Parliament in administering Maori affairs. No progress was made with this mainly because Governor George Grey was a man who kept as much power in his hands as he could. The Governor continued constitutionally to have the final say on all government affairs until 1856 when the House of Representatives assumed full responsibility for self-government, except that Grey's successor, Gore Browne, similarly felt he could handle Maori concerns separately with responsibility to the Colonial Office and without direct input from Maori themselves. (The New Zealand Government wasn't given control of Maori policy until the 1860s.)

Tamihana went to Auckland in 1855 to present a case for Maori MPs or for a council, a 'runanga', of chiefs to work side by side with Parliament. He was ungraciously ignored by the authorities and that persuaded him to support the concept of a Maori king. There was also a sense among some Maori, especially those who had travelled to England, that the British got some of their power from their unity under a single monarch.

When the idea of a Maori king did take hold in the late 1850s, the settlers, backed by the British government, saw it as a threat to their ultimate authority. The concept was supported by some enlightened British residents. Chief Justice Sir William Martin saw it as a way of representing genuine Maori interests and bringing order and calm to their representations.

Governor Gore Browne ignored advice from the Governor of New South Wales, Sir William Denison, who wrote to him: 'You have now as a fact the establishment of something analogous to a general government among the Maories, a recognition on their part of the necessity of some paramount authority: this is a step in the right direction; do not ignore it.

'Do not on the ground that some evil may spring from it, make the Natives suspicious of your motives by opposing it, but avail yourself of the opportunity to introduce some more of the elements of good government among them.'

Denison left unanswered the questions: could the government have sailed into the future in peace had it tried to use the Maori monarchy as a focus for positive negotiation? Or was it already too late for them to, Canute-like, turn back the waves of British immigrants determined to turn this into a 'civilised' agrarian colony? The idea of setting up a Maori parliament had faded during discussion between iwi leaders in the mid-1850s and that's when a group of Maori, led by Tamihana, had decided a Maori leader was needed to unify their position of protecting land tenure and rangatiratanga. They cast around for a title but eventually decided on 'king'. A number of Maori leaders did not subscribe to the kingship plan but the majority of the powerful Waikato people was enough to ensure confirmation for the Kingites.

Once the decision was made, the Kingmaker and his associates approached a number of senior chiefs who proved reluctant to take up the leadership, among them

Iwikau Te Heuheu, a Ngati Tuwharetoa chief of the Taupo region. Discussions were held on what the title should be: chief of chiefs, supreme chief, among others. Te Wherowhero, by then in his sixties, had immense prestige as a courageous former warrior and a leader of the powerful Tainui iwi and ancestral ties back to the canoe.

Te Wherowhero accepted the role of king under his taken name of Potatau I. On 1 June 1858, at Ngaruawahia, he was crowned by the brilliant and ubiquitous Wiremu Tamihana and, according to one source, the country was formally named 'Aotearoa'. Although he had never been baptised and had refused to sign the Treaty, Te Wherowhero was quoted as saying at his coronation that his people should use the new kingly position to unify Maori and 'to hold fast to love, to the law and to faith in God'.

Te Heuheu said: 'Potatau, this day I create you king of the Maori people. You and Queen Victoria shall be bound together to be one. The religion of Christ shall be the mantle of your protection; the law shall be the whariki mat for your feet, for ever and ever onward.' But Potatau's reign was short. At Ngaruawahia, he set up a council, 'Te Runanga o Ngaruawahia', to counsel him, but almost exactly two years after his accession he died.

In the traditions of monarchical succ:esson, the next king was Potatau's oldest son, Tawhiao. Potatau and his successor, and their principal adviser, Tamihana, were moderate realists and saw the new unity as a means of protecting Maori interests through their own autonomy rather than expanding them. There could be no reasonable assumption that most Tainui intended to take the country back. Also, there was dissent within Waikato iwi about the King movement, some strongly for it, some moderately so and others against even the sovereignty of Queen Victoria.

The movement's sudden emergence and the fact that Tainui had sent warriors to support Te Atiawa in Taranaki convinced Pakeha that Maori were setting up an alternative government with a new sovereign to compete with Queen Victoria's sovereignty granted under the Treaty. Governor Gore Browne predicted in 1857 that if Maori attempted to create a distinct national movement it would result eventually in 'collision'.

For Aucklanders, not far north of Ngaruawahia, the reports of continuing Maori military defiance of the government and settlers in Taranaki was disturbing enough but the possibility of an antagonistic, unified Maori movement among the populous and powerful Waikato people was alarming. Governor Browne had begun to plan an invasion of the Waikato with British troops when he was replaced by George Grey in December 1861. Grey thought at first he could perhaps mollify Maori and come to some accommodation but what he found was that, since his first term as Governor, Maori distrust of Pakeha leadership had intensified both in Taranaki and the more potentially dangerous Waikato.

Maori had come to understand that what became known as 'incremental confiscation' was depriving them of their most accessible and valuable land. There is no doubt that Grey quickly understood what Gore Browne had also known — that angry, even loosely unified Maori not far south of Auckland posed a threat to the city and thus to the colony and therefore military suppression of Maori became, in his mind, essentially the only way forward. Tawhiao was the Maori king for thirty-four tumultuous years. After the major battles of the Waikato War, he and his supporters were declared rebels and about half a million hectares of their best land confiscated.

Tawhiao and Rewi Maniapoto retreated behind the boundary of the Puniu River into what is now the King Country and forbade Europeans to cross it. The government didn't intervene and informally acknowledged the refuge of the King Country. Although the new king said the killing must be ended, he continued to argue against surveys, land courts and sales and many Pakeha institutions. In 1881, long negotiations with the government ended when Tawhiao and his followers submitted their arms to the resident magistrate at Pirongia (then Alexandra) and returned to the Waikato.

But he continued to struggle for the return of confiscated land. He travelled to England in 1884 to seek an audience with Queen Victoria in pursuit of justice for land claims. An audience was declined on the grounds that domestic issues were under the jurisdiction of the New Zealand government.

Maori kings have continued, with varying degrees of political influence: Mahuta Tawhiao, 1894–1912; Te Rata Mahuta, 1912–33; Koroki Mahuta, 1933–1966; Te Atairangikaahu, the first Maori Queen, 1966–2006; and Tuheitia Paki, 2006 — the current Maori king.

The most forceful, persuasive and influential person linked to the King movement in the twentieth century was Te Rata's niece, Te Puea Herangi. She was a powerful voice in the media and was largely responsible for many Waikato Maori refusing conscription during the First World War because of the land confiscations, fifty years before. Conscription was expanded to include Maori in 1917, but many men from the Waikato and the Ureweras refused to go to war, were arrested and served time in prison.

Chapter 6
The Waikato War

$\mathcal{T}$he British invasion of Waikato in the mild winter of 1863 led to the biggest campaign of the New Zealand Wars, the most unabashed land grab and the most ferocious drive to extinguish a shared place in the colony for Maori.

Governor Gore Browne, whose intractability had sparked the war in Taranaki, had begun to prepare for an assault on the Waikato before his term as governor expired in October 1861. His plans included the construction of a military road to the south, a move fully supported by Auckland settlers who feared an invasion — as they had during the Northern War — and had constructed strong defensive positions. They wanted the British army to strike first.

Their fear of the numerous and powerful Maori not far south was not entirely without sense. The most aggressive of the Kingites had considered two retaliatory plans as the military road was pushed southwards towards the Waikato. The first was to occupy land across the Bombay

Hills and Drury and attack military traffic. The second — and they set the date at 1 September 1861, according to journalist James Cowan — was a direct, night-time assault on Auckland from two directions. One group would assemble in the Hunuas and attack from the east and the other would move down the Waikato River, cross the Manukau, and attack from the west. The town would be set alight by Maori living there for that purpose. Pakeha — with the exception of some pre-selections — would be slaughtered. Maori in other parts of New Zealand were to be urged to rise up against Pakeha at the same time.

Such a co-ordinated move as a surprise was impractical and a large force of British soldiers could have been assembled quickly to defend the town. Also, there must have been restraints from a strong moderate group of chiefs within the King movement who wanted justice but without the kind of violence that would totally disrupt any negotiations over land and mana.

Fort Britomart was built on a promontory that soared out over the edge of the southern shore of the Waitemata Harbour, the steep cliff more than 12 metres above the sea. It was first known as Flagstaff Hill because the Royal Standard was flown from there to celebrate the purchase of the town site from Ngati Whatua in 1840. Then it became Point Britomart after HMS *Britomart*, which surveyed the Waitemata when the capital was moved south from Russell. By 1863, at the open Princes Street end — with cliffs on the other three sides — a stockade had been built and was protected by a fearsome array of artillery. (Britomart Point was later laboriously shovelled away to reclaim land along the harbour's edge below and now slopes away down Emily Place from the northern end of Princes Street.) Another major blockhouse was in the area now centred on Albert Park. Sentries were in place and volunteers patrolled the city where Maori were under curfew.

According to Cowan, the Kingite invasion plan was abandoned when the news was received that George Grey was returning as Governor and, they believed, would consider their political aspirations more sympathetically.

It's impossible to get inside Grey's psyche — from what he wrote and what has been written about him — after he arrived back for his second term as Governor in December 1861. He certainly had an interest in Maori and their traditions and some empathy. He proposed alternative ways to encourage Maori desire for rangatiratanga through runanga that had been partially adopted in some places, most prominently under the supervision of Grey confidant John Gorst, but he sensed greater suspicion and mistrust of Pakeha among them.

It's fair to say, I think, that although he talked of peace and compromise there is not much evidence that he deeply believed in it, with work continuing on Gore Browne's military road south, which he must have known was a provocation. He was driven by increasing settler numbers, impatience with the King movement among members of the House of Representatives and an ambitious desire to impose dramatic closure on a situation that was troubling the Colonial Office. Quite soon, he had convinced himself that the Maori attempt at unity under a king was a dangerous division of power that broke their agreement under the Treaty to accept Queen Victoria of Great Britain as their sovereign.

Many Maori, even in the Waikato, had sought peace and others had attempted compromise, but most finally joined the more intractable members of the King movement in a bid to save their land and a place in the sun for Maori in the Waikato, Bay of Plenty and Ureweras. The war lasted for a year and many North Island iwi sent warriors in support and provided food and logistical back-up for the combatants.

As the military road moved ominously southwards, all Maori living and working from South Auckland to the Waikato border were required to make an oath of loyalty to the Queen. Many moved south to join the Kingitanga movement and others were forced to, as Cowan put it: 'The process of ejection of those natives who could not abandon their fellow-countrymen was now carried out at the Manukau, Papakura, Patumahoe, Tuakau and other districts between Auckland and the frontier waters. The principal iwi evicted was Ngati Pou who had a settlement on the right (north) bank of the Waikato at Tuakau with large cultivations of food crops and fruit groves.'

One of the saddest effects of the war on Maori, both

in Taranaki and, even more so, in the Waikato, was that Maori had eagerly and competently embraced the cultivation of temperate-zone crops and farm animals Pakeha had brought with them. Life had been hard for Maori for centuries with minimal carbohydrate, based mainly on fern root. One can imagine the relish with which they found that potatoes Pakeha brought with them thrived and sometimes yielded two crops a year. And imagine the delight with which they adopted maize, peaches and apples and other bountiful plants. Quite quickly, peach trees sprang up wherever Maori lived.

From the 1840s until the end of the 1850s, the Waikato and Bay of Plenty were extraordinarily productive. In 1849, Governor George Grey visited the Waikato and wrote to the Secretary of State for the Colonies in London: 'Altogether I have not seen a more thriving or contented population in any part of the world.' He noted that 'the natives' have, at one place, more than four hundred hectares in wheat, 'good orchards with fruit trees of the best kind, grafted and budded by themselves', as well as extensive cultivations of Indian corn and potatoes and 'a considerable number of horses and horned stock'.

In 1857, Attorney-General William Swainson wrote that the districts of Bay of Plenty, Taupo and Rotorua had about twelve hundred hectares in wheat, eight hundred hectares in maize and more than four hundred hectares in kumara. They owned nearly a thousand horses, two hundred head of cattle, five thousand pigs, four water-mills and ninety-six ploughs. Swainson added that they owned forty-three small coasting vessels and about nine hundred canoes. Cowan wrote that 'long before the Waikato war, travellers [to Te Awamutu, Rangiaowhia, Kihikihi and Orakau] found there to their astonishment many beautiful settlements, with large fields of wheat, potatoes and maize arranged in neat streets, shaded by groves of peach and apple trees. Each large village had its water-driven flour-mill procured by the community, which after harvest was kept busily grinding into flour the abundant yield of cornfields.'

A tough, disputatious Scottish settler, Dr S. M. Martin, who was for a while editor of the *New Zealand Herald*, remarked as early as 1845 that Maori 'produced food so cheaply they would ruin the white settlers' market'. He also wrote presciently: 'The white settler had his own place for Maori in the scheme of things, and it was certainly not that of a competitor. The Maori was expected to be the willing accomplice into converting his forests into white man's farms.'

By the time war came in 1863 the causes nowadays seem to be clear enough. After the first Taranaki War, Wiremu Kingi became a guest of the powerful fighting chief Rewi Maniapoto. A number of Waikato warriors had died in Wiremu Kingi's campaign over ownership of the Waitara block near New Plymouth, so Waikato Maori would have had few allusions about what was at stake, knowing of the encroachment and continuing confiscation of land in Taranaki. They would have been aware too of military settlers, many recruited in Australia, waiting in Auckland or building the military road south.

Any hope that they would be allowed significant say in governing themselves or their resources disappeared once Grey continued the military road south from Drury. When it reached Mangatawhiri, Maori considered it a declaration of war.

In fact, as the road progressed south and General Duncan Cameron assembled a large and growing army for the drive into the Waikato, he was held up by continuing guerrilla attacks on his supply lines. He was forced to use more and more of his troops to build and man blockhouses on the route south as Maori raiding parties disrupted movement along the road and had no compunction about killing settlers and their families in the region.

Four days before the British Army moved on from Mangatawhiri and marched on a Maori defensive position at Meremere, Grey sent a letter to the 'Chiefs of Waikato' in which he listed their crimes: 'You are now assembling in armed bands; you are constantly threatening to come down the river to ravage the Settlement of Auckland and to murder peaceable settlers . . . '

The letter ended with a threat that probably made the Kingites more determined to fight: 'Those who wage war against Her Majesty, or remain in arms, threatening the lives of Her peaceable subjects, must take the consequences of their acts, and they must understand that they will forfeit the right to the possession of their lands guaranteed to them by the Treaty of Waitangi, which kinds will be occupied by a population capable of protecting for the future the quiet and unoffending from the violence from which they are now so constantly threatened.'

Cameron, with his army of mostly professional British soldiers, moved first against a powerful defensive pa at Meremere in his bid for a comprehensive victory that would destroy the Kingite army. It looked as though Maori might at last have the numbers with an estimated one thousand men at the well-made defensive structure. Cameron had a small fleet of river vessels to carry men and supplies to launch his attack. One of them, the purpose-built, iron-plated, paddle-steamer gunboat, *Pioneer*, was the New Zealand government's first naval vessel, built in Sydney and towed across the Tasman for just such a task as carrying the attack on Maori along the Waikato River. It could carry three hundred men and, along with another, smaller, paddle-steamer, the *Avon*, brought Cameron's assault troops towards Meremere. The *Avon* had been built in Sydney and assembled in Auckland.

It was an anti-climax. Cameron was in a position to attack the pa from both north and south and outflank the defenders who were not slow to realise their position was essentially vulnerable and abandoned the pa.

Cameron and Grey needed a hammer-blow to end the war quickly and hoped it would come at Rangiriri (on a battlefield now severed by the motorway south from Auckland, not far from the present town). The British launched a well-planned attack on a strongly constructed defensive position on the banks of the Waikato River. Its earthworks ranged along a ridge between Lake Waikare at the rear and the river. It was a solid structure with ditches and concealed rifle pits along the sides, and a central fortress that seemed impregnable. But once the outer defences had been overwhelmed this central blockhouse was surrounded. From then on, after the first day, it was only a matter of time. A defensive structure that could well have been capable of repelling attacks even by determined, well-organised soldiers was inadequately manned.

Cameron reconnoitred the terrain and the pa from the river aboard the *Pioneer* on 18 November and began the assault two days later. The first day proved costly for the British but a disaster also looked imminent for Maori. Cameron had eight hundred and sixty men in his attacking force backed by another six hundred men nearby. Artillery both on land and aboard gunboats on the river pounded Maori positions for about two hours but made little impression on the earthworks although defenders in the trenches and rifle-pits suffered from accurate shelling.

The bombardment was suspended as the British troops began their assault and took the first line of defence with a bayonet charge. The cost in casualties was high on both sides. Several determined assaults on the central redoubt on the crest of the ridge were beaten back and the day ended in an impasse.

It had become clear that apart from the central blockade the number of defenders was inadequate, partly because of lack of coordination among Maori taua (war parties). Warrior dispositions around the province were difficult to arrange and after Meremere some went back to their homes. King Tawhiao and Wiremu Tamihana were both present but were spirited away during the first night after initial British assaults when defeat became likely. They were protected as they left by bodyguards, further depleting the defending force.

The morning after the original assaults, as the British began to mount a new series of attacks, defenders raised a white flag in a bid to seek negotiation, they claimed later, but it was taken as surrender by the British who immediately occupied the pa. The casualties were high — about forty-five killed on each side, but nearly two hundred Maori were taken prisoner, including a number of their leaders. The prisoners were taken to Kawau Island in the Hauraki Gulf (from where they escaped less than a year later).

Rangiriri was perhaps the defining battle of the Waikato War. It opened up the region for the British to move forward and, initially, they had the resources to do so swiftly. A week later, Cameron had occupied the Maori king's capital at Ngaruawahia and Tawhiao had retreated to the sanctuary of the King Country. There was hard fighting to come but victory looked closer to Cameron than it had early in November. Grey, building up all the personal credit he could, told London: 'There can, I think, be no doubt that the neck of this unhappy rebellion is now broken.'

Cameron and his army slowed up after the initial thrust, struggling with logistical difficulties. His was a huge army and keeping it supplied and the supply chain protected was a considerable exercise.

At Paterangi, Rewi Maniapoto had overseen the building of the largest and, on the face of it, the most powerful fighting pa of them all and one estimate was that it had two thousand men ready to defend it. But despite attempts by provocative skirmishes, the British had decided not to confront it but to outflank it and capture Rangiaowhia, the fertile Kingite breadbasket beyond. This was made possible by the offer of guidance from a part-Maori guide who had lived at Paterangi. He led a large force around the pa late at night. They travelled in silence, their swords and other equipment muffled. Cameron then moved against the unprotected fields of Rangiaowhia.

James Cowan wrote: 'The large unfortified settlement of Rangiaowhia came in sight, a scene of peace and beauty. Fields of wheat maize and potatoes extended over long slender slopes, and peach-groves shading clutches of thatched houses were scattered along a green hill trending north and south, the crown of the village, with the steeples of two churches rising above the trees a quarter of a mile apart.'

Some Maori in the 'thatched houses' fled but others stayed and fought and were ruthlessly killed, including a number of non-combatants. The houses were set alight and the village destroyed. This added to Maori sadness and fury. They struggled away with what food and supplies they could carry.

Rewi Maniapoto moved about four hundred warriors to the Hairini ridge, between Te Awamutu and Rangiaowhia, to make time for more food supplies to be removed by Maori from Rangiaowhia. It was folly. The British attacked with twelve hundred men, flushed out the defenders and took to them with their bayonets. The Forest Rangers and other units then carried away as much loot as they could back to their base at Te Awamutu.

Cameron's brilliant clandestine night-time move around Paterangi, with his three thousand men, avoiding yet another attritional fixed battle against a well-fortified pa, effectively gave him control over the Waikato basin with its fertile plain. His rout of the defenders at Hairini had delivered a dramatic blow to Kingites. Any hope that Maori could prevail died on the Hairini ridge.

The British built a redoubt at Paterangi, and had close to seven thousand troops in the area, most of them based in Te Awamutu. But Cameron, constantly prodded by Grey, was restless for a coup de grace, a decisive rout that would overwhelm the Kingite cause and allow British rule to expand into the Waikato and clear the way for the military settlers who, it was planned, would basically garrison the region, with Maori pushed back into the King Country.

Wiremu Tamihana, ever the mediator when the chance came, wrote to Grey and to other Maori leaders pushing for peace negotiations. He was ignored, as he was later when he tried for mediation as the war moved to the Bay of Plenty. The British were no longer interested in compromise. But there was one fight they hadn't foreseen. They won it in the field but lost it in the song and story of the nation.

The battle of Orakau was the stuff that myths are made from — and quite rightly so. It was the most famous battle of the New Zealand Wars and the story of Maori courage and determination in the face of overwhelming odds has been remembered ever since. It was after Orakau that the Waikato Kingites withdrew completely into what is today known as the King Country.

Orakau inspired one of the country's earliest feature films, *Rewi's Last Stand* (1925), reshot and reissued with sound in 1940, both times by Rudall Hayward. A novel of the same name written from the film script by Hayward and A. W. Reed (who was also the publisher) was released in 1939.

About three hundred Maori — perhaps two-thirds of

them fighting men — held out for three days in a hastily built, incomplete pa in a peach grove at Orakau. From 31 March to 2 April 1864, they repulsed repeated assaults from more than a thousand British soldiers. They were led by Rewi Maniapoto but most of the defenders were Tuhoe (down from the Urewera hills to honour a mutual obligation), Hawke's Bay's Ngati Kahungunu, Ngati Raukawa of Waikato and Taupo with some warriors from other iwi.

Ngati Raukawa and especially Tuhoe wanted a show of defiance against the British, encamped at Kihikihi less than four kilometres away. They chose to build the pa even though Rewi Maniapoto, their general, was aware of the fatal flaws in the site: it was easily surrounded (which it soon was) and without access to water. The great Maori fighting pa were built in terrain that provided a water source and an avenue for escape into the bush.

The pa under construction was discovered by a surveyor. Brigadier-General George Carey, officer in charge of the British troops at Kihikihi, was informed and rode over to take a look. Believing the pa to be incomplete and vulnerable, he decided on a quick assault to destroy it. The British troops, ferociously disciplined, charged three times. They suffered severe losses as the Maori defenders cut them down. Although the odds were staggeringly in favour of the British, Carey understood that this could be the defining defeat in the war; so he sought reinforcements from General

Duncan Cameron. About five hundred reinforcements and Cameron himself arrived.

After three days, out of water, low on ammunition and having repelled five assaults, the game was up for Rewi and his warriors but they still refused to concede defeat, and so did the women and children. Offered a chance to surrender, they famously declared they would fight on 'ake, ake, ake', forever, forever, forever.

A version of the negotiations that led to that legend was told at Parliament buildings in Wellington twenty-four years later by Ngati Raukawa chief, Hitiri Te Paerata, who was among the defenders of the pa and whose father had been responsible for designing the fortifications. He began his story with: 'I feel somewhat confused and embarrassed having to meet all these members of Parliament and ladies, more especially as we were defeated at the fight you now ask me to give you an account of; but if it will please you I will endeavour to do so.' He described the battle and then said that about midday on the third day they were suffering critically from lack of water and running out of ammunition. Then Major Gilbert Mair (who, interestingly, was interpreting for Te Paerata during his 1888 speech at Parliament) was sent by Cameron to negotiate a surrender.

Mair was one of the most extraordinary Pakeha colonials involved in the New Zealand Wars. Not only could he speak Te Reo, he had a profound knowledge of tikanga (Maori traditions and customs). Later in his career he became a government interpreter, a land purchase officer, a surveyor, a farmer, and a botanist, but most famously a soldier — commander of the kupapa No 1 Arawa Flying Column with which he spent some years tracking and fighting Te Kooti. His biography, written by Ron Crosby, was entitled *Gilbert Mair: Te Kooti's Nemesis.*

Te Paerata continued: 'He [Mair] came up to within a few yards of where we were, our men all aiming at him with their guns, and said, "Let the fighting cease, because you are surrounded. Your position is hopeless. If you persist in fighting you will all be killed, and your women and children will die with you."

'This word was sent around, and all the chiefs and people within the pa took counsel on the General's message . . . What we proposed was that the troops should go away with all their dead and wounded, and we would also go away with ours. These negotiations lasted about half an hour before our ultimatum had been decided upon. Then the General sent Major Mair, who said, "Let the women and children be sent out; we will protect them so that they may not die."

'Then up rose my sister, Ahumai, among the women and said, "If our husbands and brothers are to die what profit is it to us that we should live? Let us die with the men." Seeing that the women were all of one mind, then Hapurona, Rewi and my father said "Ake, ake, ake". The people repeated these words with a great shout, and one of my people named Wereta fired at Major Mair, hitting him on the top of the right shoulder. Of course, this treacherous work broke off the negotiations, and the firing commenced on both sides more furiously than ever . . . '

The besieged finally made a fighting retreat and, although some were cut down by cavalry as they went, many, including Rewi, made their escape. As historian James Belich says: 'It says a great deal for the nerve of Rewi and his associates that they did not allow even this desperate expedient to become uncontrolled. The Maoris advanced in a compact body with the women and children in the centre and the best warriors in the front. Most men had reserved a few rounds for such an eventually, but the column at first held its fire and advanced in perfect silence.'

The British soldiers were preoccupied building a sap to the wall of the pa and the silent, organised retreat seemed to disconcert others. They moved a few hundred metres and broke through a line of soldiers at cost to both sides. But a small cavalry unit and some Forest Rangers caught up with them and killed many as they fled.

It was an epic of fortitude, which, like many Maori demonstrations of tactical and psychological superiority during the wars, confused the British and especially the colonists for whom it was essential to believe that, with courage and discipline, they were bringing enlightenment and civilisation to a backward people.

A dispatch from Orakau by a correspondent of Auckland's *Daily Southern Cross* newspaper, published on 6 April, a few days after the battle, has always represented for me the extraordinary moral and intellectual ambivalence of settlers in their need to justify their theft of land and suppression of Maori rights as a sort of crusading gift from a people more civilised and decent — while being forced to acknowledge that in many ways Maori were at least their equal.

The *Daily Southern Cross* correspondent wrote: 'When Brigadier-General Carey took up a position in front of this pa, he was enabled to dispose of his forces in such a way as to render the escape of the enemy almost impossible. The nature of the ground favoured this disposition of the attacking force; and to all appearance the natives had got themselves into a trap from which escape was impossible. But surrounded as they were, they did not surrender. Attacked by superior numbers aided by all the appliances of war, they did not yield, but . . . they were determined to fight out to the very last.

'They were also without water, and their sufferings must have been intense. To their assailants their destruction must have appeared certain; yet they rejected terms of peace, and so a sap was pushed vigorously to within five yards of the pa, hand grenades were pitched in and six-pounder guns sent grape shot among them at a range of 20 yards. They could not hold out against such fearful odds, but neither did they dream of a flag of truce. At the crisis of their fate they burst from their pa, on the western side, traversed the ground covered by the headquarter companies of the 40th Regiment . . . and made good their retreat into the swamp beyond.

'We pay no unwilling tribute to the defenders of the Orakau pa; we believe they behaved as well as any body of men could behave; and whatever we may think of their cause, they deserved to escape.'

He then immediately attacks the disposition of the artillery, and 'the conduct of the troops that allowed them to escape through their lines in broad daylight . . . We withhold censure [he doesn't] until we can ascertain the full details of the transaction which snatched a crowning victory from the hands of a gallant commanding officer and turned it into a humiliating defeat.'

He then goes on to advocate starvation of Maori as the ally of civilisation, and praises a plan to deprive them of food. 'If no rest is allowed them to get fresh plantations formed, these ten thousand at all events may be subdued. This is terrible, but war is never anything else, and anarchy is the most trouble of all . . . starvation must help us if we are to win in any reasonable time. Our words sound cruel, but it is only in sound. The real cruelty is in prolonging the struggles of a worn-out barbarian. Let the barbarian be put down by any means, however painful, and the people who were barbarians, but are now teachable, may be saved — and only so can they be saved.'

And there ends the lesson of mad moral confusion.

Interestingly, the film *Rewi's Last Stand* and the novel are both excruciatingly sentimental and patronising to Maori. While they give heroic credit to Rewi, the story is told from the point of view of a Pakeha, a young settler/Forest Ranger in love with a part-Maori woman who chooses to stay in the pa at Orakau.

A sample of the dialogue in the novel:

'You have done your best, sir. You've given them flour-mills and schools but they won't respond. At heart they're still savages.'

[Governor Grey] 'Not all of them, Regan. They are a fine people. And don't forget some of them write to us and warn us of our danger. Always remember, in dealing with aboriginal people, England must be more than just — even generous.'

This snatch of dialogue fairly accurately reflects the Pakeha attitude towards the New Zealand Wars, towards Maori and towards the history of colonisation that lasted in history and fiction for a century.

The first settlers in any numbers to move onto the confiscated land — to farm and be ready to defend the growing towns from any resurgence of Maori to re-take their land — were members of the Waikato Militia, recruited in Otago and Australia. They were granted a little under half a hectare in a nearby town they were expected to garrison, and twenty hectares as a farm.

They were provided with army food rations for a year. The land would be freehold after they had farmed it for three years. Many didn't last that long because breaking in the predominantly peatland with a nuclear family was too hard. When they left, speculating land companies moved in and bought title. They, in turn, failed because development costs were higher than expected.

A problem was that close to a hundred thousand hectares of Waikato was peatland, much of which was surveyed and settled. It was unsuitable for pastoral farming — until the subtleties of irrigation were developed. It wasn't until the twentieth century, when railway networks advanced and drainage trench techniques were beginning to be understood, that dairying emerged in the region. From the 1920s, solid agricultural growth began but it wasn't until the 1950s, that government-backed scientific research rapidly brought the extraordinary agricultural wealth of Waikato today.

Chapter 7
Bay of Plenty

General Cameron, still in search of a final blow to end the campaign in the Waikato, was instrumental in shifting the focus to the Bay of Plenty. He sent troops and warships to Tauranga (then known as Te Papa) where the harbour had become a supply route in support of the Waikato.

The district was providing warriors to fight for the Kingites in the Waikato, and taua from the East Coast were crossing through Te Papa on their way to the battlefields.

In January 1864, more than six hundred troops, under the command of Lieutenant-Colonel Henry Harper Greer, moved into the small town and a British warship, the HMS *Miranda* blockaded the harbour.

On his first visit, James Cook didn't see the harbour entrance at Te Papa but he noted that the Maori population along the Bay of Plenty coast was extremely dense. The first known European visitors to sail into the harbour were aboard the mission schooner, *Herald*, in 1828. They saw a thousand canoes, large and small, along the shore, according to Gilbert Mair, son of the man who helped build the *Herald* and was captain on the vessel for this early voyage and many others. Mair Senior was an enterprising Scottish-born trader, one of the first engaged in kauri gum exporting. Missionary Henry Williams was aboard and held a Christian service at the largest pa in the vicinity, Otamataha. During the 1830s a trade in flax built up and an Anglican missionary settled there late in the decade.

Preceding and following the arrival of British troops, correspondence swirled around the enterprise among Premier Frederick Whitaker, Colonial Secretary William Fox — both perennial figures in the shifting shape of government at that time — Native Secretary Edward Shortland and Governor Grey. Most of it involved estimating the degree of Kingite support in the Bay of Plenty. Brigadier-General George Carey declared he would take the cattle and destroy the crops of all Maori to the west of Te Papa, because of the level of Kingite support there.

The Civil Commissioner for the province, M. T. H. Smith, had the temerity to write to Carey: 'I am satisfied that any such indiscriminate seizure, and destruction of property, would inflict injury upon many innocent persons, and that its effect would be to increase the number of the disaffected, to precipitate hostilities here and to induce other iwi to take up arms, who might otherwise remain quiet.' That was on 22 January. Grey and Fox were conciliatory but after a month had passed, Mr Smith received a long letter of rebuke from Mr Shortland, which included: 'The Government can see in the facts of the case, as now explained by you, no ground for your taking the responsibility of urging Carey to suspend the intended action, which by those instructions he was directed to take.'

Local iwi, Ngai Te Rangi, supporting the Kingites in Waikato, returned as soon as they heard of the troops arriving at Te Papa. After building fortified pa on other sites, they settled on the construction of a pa on the Pukehinahina ridge only five kilometres from the British camp. It was an oblong, 80 metres long and eighteen wide. The site is enshrined in history as 'Gate Pa', so-named because it was near the gate in a post-and-rail fence above a ditch originally built by Maori to signify the edge of the town and the beginning of their land.

The main pa was designed by Pene Taka Tuaia who, according to one source, learnt his military engineering skills under Kawiti during the Northern War. Timber was scarce in the Te Papa district so the palisade was built of manuka stakes, and posts and rails taken from a settler's stock yard and from fences near the British camp. It had an outer fence to impede soldiers on the charge but the stockade was not as robust as in other pa constructed to repel British army assaults. A smaller adjacent pa was not quite finished by the time the battle began but it was part of a double-redoubt illusion.

Bunkers were small but interconnected with others and with outer trenches and rifle-pits. They were small to ensure that if a shell broke through the wooden and earth-topped roofs only a few occupants would be affected. This ruse succeeded because even after the massive bombardment, only fifteen of the two hundred Maori had been killed.

Ngai Te Rangi assumed that ultimately the British would attack and tried to incite them. They had neither the numbers to launch even a surprise assault on the British base nor would they have had any chance of winning a battle in the open, as their subsequent disaster at Te Ranga underlined.

Women helped build the pa but were sent back to the villages before the fighting began — except for a part-European woman warrior, Heni te Kiri Karamu, known as Heni Pore, who had proved her worth in bush-fighting adventures.

A curious preamble to the battle was a set of chivalric rules (according to an account written by Gilbert Mair Junior, some years later) that civilians would not be interfered with; that soldiers captured would be disarmed and handed over to 'the authorities'; that 'even if armed and fled through fear to the House of God or a priest they would not be followed'; that the wounded would be treated with kindness and the dead would not be mutilated. These rules 'were written out by an enlightened mission student, Henare Taratoa who had been educated by Archdeacon (afterwards Bishop) Hadfield of Otaki'.

The Ngai Te Rangi chief, Rawiri Puhirake, began issuing challenges to the British inviting them to attack, saying he had built the pa close to the British base to allow the soldiers to be fresh when they arrived. He would build a road for them if they wished. It was bravado but with the purpose of urging the British on because he had the pa well supplied and his men in place and ready. He needed the battle sooner rather than later, although he was awaiting the arrival of reinforcements from the East Coast.

But for Rawiri and his two hundred and thirty warriors, the odds suddenly changed dramatically. Greer had kept him waiting because Cameron saw a chance of a major victory against Kingites supporters. He arrived with reinforcements and had available about seventeen hundred men by the time the fighting began. Rawiri's support from the East Coast was abruptly halted at Maketu where they were beaten back by a British unit and a taua of Te Arawa, who supported the government and with whom Ngai Te Rangi had been at war during the 1830s.

At Gate Pa, the British stood off behind a prolonged artillery bombardment that James Belich described as 'of unprecedented intensity' and it was by far the heaviest of the New Zealand Wars. In action were twenty-four-pounder howitzers, and the relatively new and especially dangerous Armstrong guns. The guns opened fire for an hour on the afternoon of 28 January and the next day the bombardment began at dawn and continued until 4 p.m. The cannon and mortars aimed to drop shells behind the palisade into the pa in a bid to kill as many Maori as possible. The barrage was also aimed at one corner of the main redoubt to create a major breach as target for an assault party. The noise and concussion within the pa must have been shattering for the defenders even though they were taking refuge in their underground bunkers.

The cannon breached the palisade, leaving a major gap. Steady summer rain had drenched the area when Cameron — convinced the toll on the Maori by the bombardment would have basically incapacitated any organised defence — sent a party of three hundred assault troops on a frontal attack. Half of them were from the Naval Brigade (famously dangerous on the attack) and from the 43rd Regiment. As they charged, four abreast, they were backed by support groups numbering about five hundred men, some of whom were assigned to provide small arms fire to cover the attackers. They met almost no resistance as they broke into the pa. All had gone according to Cameron's meticulous plan.

It was a trap. A few minutes later the British attackers came stampeding away from the pa, panic-stricken. The defenders — with almost unbelievable resilience and discipline — had sat out the bombardment in their intricate series of linked bunkers, waited until the assault part was inside and above them and unleashed a fusillade from short range that killed thirty-one and wounded eighty of the soldiers (ten of them officers) in a few minutes. Most of the British assault party saw few of their enemy and had little chance to respond.

Had the East Coast allies arrived and had Rawiri Puhirake decided to immediately pursue the fleeing soldiers with all his warriors, he could conceivably have destroyed the British force at Tauranga. This thought had certainly been entertained by Cameron. In his report to Grey, he wrote: 'On my arrival at the spot I considered it inadvisable to renew the assault, and directed a line of entrenchments to be thrown up within one hundred yards so as to be able to maintain our position and resume operations the following morning.' According to another account, Cameron 'waited anxiously [at the entrenchments] for daylight'.

An account given forty years later by a Ngai Te Rangi chief, Hori Ngatai who survived the battle, 'to a number of distinguished officials, including several Members of Parliament', appeared in a booklet published by the *Bay of Plenty Times* in 1926. His story seems detached but rather romanticised by time: 'Through and over the breach walls they rushed; they entered the ruins of the larger pa; most of it was in their possession. But all at once the tide of war was changed. Up leapt our men from the rifle pits as if vomited from the bowels of the earth, and together with those who had been forced back by the 68th Regiment in the rear, began a deadly hand-to-hand fight with the storming party . . . '

A number of other explanations have been offered for the rout at Gate Pa, for the flight of normally disciplined, battle-hardened soldiers but they seem muddled and unconvincing. Only the trap theory of James Belich makes sense. Once the officers were cut down by largely unseen assailants, the men became disorientated and terrified, and fled. Cameron gets close to understanding what happened. In his report to Governor Grey, he wrote: 'This repulse I am at a loss to explain otherwise than by attributing it to the confusion created among the men by the intricate nature of the interior defences, and the sudden fall of so many of their officers.'

It was the most devastating defeat experienced by the British during the course of the New Zealand Wars. They had been beaten before, but never quite like this. Maori lost twenty-five killed and an unknown number of wounded over the two days. Before the battle began the 68th Regiment had found a way around the swamps on both sides of the pa and took up a position in the rear to cut off any Maori escape. But, during that night, the warriors still managed to abandon the pa and slip away, largely unnoticed.

The British made a plan of the Gate Pa fortifications and used it as a potential model for the trench warfare that underpinned so much of the fighting in the First World War.

Incidental to Gate Pa was a battle at Maketu. The reinforcements Rawiri Puhirake expected from the East Coast — about seven hundred of them according to one account — were anticipated by a small contingent of British troops, plus men from local militia and the New Zealand Defence Force. They built a substantial redoubt on a hilltop from which they hoped to intercept the reinforcements, and installed two six-pounder Armstrong field guns. The Maori party was large enough to surround the redoubt. They began digging a sap, covering themselves from the redoubt with small arms fire.

The next day two heavily armed British naval vessels arrived, HMS *Esk*, which had taken Cameron to Te Papa, and HMS *Falcon*. They moved in close to the shore from where they shelled the Maori digging the sap. Then the Arawa force arrived. Together they turned the East Coast warriors back.

The report of the sap inspired an editorial attempt at humour in Auckland's *Daily Southern Cross:* 'It is hardly a month since we reduced to extremity, and might, but for an error, have secured the whole garrison of Orakau pa. The means employed was a sap, a mode of warfare not especially a favourite with the people of New Zealand, but has obviously advantages of its own when rightly applied . . . We learn that when the *Falcon* arrived to shell the natives from their position they had run a sap to within eighty yards of the redoubt, within which were the British forces . . .

'It is absurd enough to think of and picture to ourselves a party of British soldiers within a redoubt, seeing their dusky foes putting into practice, in a quaint half-civilised way of their own, the lesson in military science they had just been taught in no very easy school [at Orakau]. We can imagine the mingled disgust and surprise of the veterans, who had ever dreamt of such a thing — and small wonder when history has not, so far as we know, a parallel case — at seeing a business-like sap driven by an amateur corps of sappers and miners under the direction of a copper-coloured engineer officer in a highly primitive uniform . . .

'We have now been fighting in this Province for nine months, and we have not made the Maori afraid of us. It is not pleasant to say this because our wonted experience in war is very different . . . ' The writer went on to say that other nations are afraid of British bayonets but 'the natives of New Zealand have fought again and again against the choicest troops of the British army, led by a general of name and fame, and they are by no means afraid to do so again. The question, how is this? is more easily asked than answered.'

Cameron got his victory two months later. On 21 June, Greer and a patrol of nearly six hundred men discovered about five hundred of Puhirake's men (including allies from Ngati Rangiwewehi (Rotorua), Ngati Pikiao

(Rotoiti) and Ngati Porou) beginning the construction of another pa at Te Ranga. He called for reinforcements and at last the British were able to fight a battle on their terms — in the open where they could use their superior numbers and their tried, trusted, traditional tactics. One hundred and six Maori died around their trenches, among them the hero of Gate Pa, Rawiri Puhirake, and Henare Taratoa, the young teacher who composed the code of battle conduct before the Gate Pa battle began.

The Bay of Plenty campaign was virtually over. British morale was restored, especially for the 43rd Regiment whose members had fled from the terror of Gate Pa and been blamed for cowardice. They were triumphant at Te Ranga, fighting a battle they understood.

A month later, a group of Ngai Te Rangi warriors surrendered to the British and, by the end of August, the iwi had given in. Just over twenty thousand hectares of land was confiscated. The government supplied Maori with seeds and with food until their crops were harvested.

The battle of Gate Pa was the ultimate example of the British underestimating the quality of the Maori mind and temperament — almost two decades after Ohaeawai. It probably had something to do with the power of words to shape a cast of mind. Politicians, settlers, soldiers and newspaper correspondents had the word 'savages' embedded in their minds as a synonym for Maori, even in the context of some admiration. It recurs in almost every Pakeha discussion on Maori life and culture.

One newspaper correspondent, on the eve of the Waikato War, appealed for more troops: 'A large accession to our numbers would have a salutary effect. It would restore confidence, which some have sought to undermine, and what is of much greater moment after all, it would enable General Cameron to make short work of the savages, who force upon us a war of races.'

Even when they were out-thought and outfought, Pakeha almost always spread the blame among themselves and blocked the concept of defeat by the 'savages'. By holding that word in their heads they instinctively regarded Maori as irrational, excitable and violently undisciplined. In fact, one newspaper correspondent wrote: 'A native taken unawares, or at close range, becomes too excited to take deliberate aim, whereas the trained Englishman can take cover and fire with unerring effect.' On occasions 'barbarians' was used — people with no understanding of morality or decency.

The fact that Maori refused to stand and fight in the open and face a bayonet charge confirmed this mental image. The reality was that Maori understood early in the war in the North that facing a highly disciplined enemy charging at you in much greater numbers on open ground with rifle and bayonet when you were armed with a muzzle-loading rifle and a long-handled tomahawk was a short-cut back to Hawaiki.

Bush-fighting was almost always inconclusive and the old defensive pa of tribal wars with two palisades perched on inaccessible high ground, preferably with cliffs over water on three sides and no escape route could not be defended against artillery. Language betrays a frame of mind. Maori were said to 'infest' the bush in the words of more than one commentator. He also wrote: 'One can readily perceive how vastly superior civilized men, animated with these feelings [comradeship in arms], are to the savage race to whom they are opposed.'

So Ngapuhi engineers — Kawiti was the original designer — produced the modern pa set in the right terrain with stockades that could withstand cannon, which often had to be hauled laboriously through the bush. The stockades were mostly constructed from stout tree trunks, and water and an escape route into the bush were tactically essential.

The almost impregnable forts worked admirably in the north, on occasions in Taranaki, and at Gate Pa. The concept held up for a while at Orakau, where it failed in the end because there were so few defenders, no water and no safe escape route.

Chapter 8
The Throes of Two Great Warriors

During the great battles in Taranaki, the Waikato and Bay of Plenty in the opening years of the 1860s, the economic base of many Maori communities had been either neglected because of the absence of warriors or deliberately destroyed by British soldiers.

Although the Pakeha commentary at the time (and often for the next century) described Maori in the mid-1860s as 'sullen' or even as 'sulking', there was still unease among settlers who knew Maori were far from defeated and dispirited.

Local skirmishes continued between the races and Maori continued to fight among themselves, settling inter-tribal disputes often involving their complex relationship with Pakeha. But if the government and settlers thought the big battles were over, they were mistaken. Two major military leaders arose late in the decade to shatter any complacency or composure: Riwha Titokowaru in Taranaki/Whanganui, and Te Kooti Arikirangi in Poverty Bay and the Ureweras.

Titokowaru has been called 'arguably the greatest general New Zealand has produced' by one historian and lauded by others since, and yet he was virtually written out of our history for most of a century. Only James Cowan of the late nineteenth and early twentieth century historians gave Titokowaru any of the sustained attention he deserved — until historian James Belich unearthed the true story of a charismatic man and brilliant military strategist who had control of Taranaki for several months.

Cowan writes in detail about Titokowaru and his south Taranaki campaign but with heavy emphasis on the barbarism and fanaticism of his 'Hauhau' followers rather than on his cause and his tactical genius. Maori opposing the local militias were referred to dismissively as 'Hauhaus' from then on until the demise of Te Kooti in the early 1870s. This helped government and settlers from having to identify and cope morally with their cause.

Titokowaru was a spiritual leader, highly imaginative and intuitive and, at the same time, intelligent and pragmatic. He belonged to the Ngati Manuhiakai hapu of Ngati Ruanui, in southern Taranaki. Ngati Ruanui had long been wary of land sales to the European settlers and had been battlefield supporters of Wiremu Kingi of Te Atiawa. All his life, Titokowaru fluctuated between the advocacy of peace and the perceived need for war. He was involved in skirmishes against the British in the early 1840s but then was baptised as a Methodist. He learnt to write in Maori during this period, became deeply involved in Bible studies and, by 1850, was living in Patea as an assistant Methodist teacher, preaching peace.

In the early 1850s, he became a Maori nationalist, supporting the campaign to establish a Maori king and increasingly opposing land sales to settlers. It's certain that he took part in the wars and skirmishes of the early 1860s when he was wounded and lost the sight in his right eye.

In 1866, he became a persuasive advocate for peace, having come under the influence of Te Ua Haumene, the founder of Pai Marire, whose followers were known for a long time as 'Hauhaus'. Titokowaru grafted elements of Christianity into his form of mysticism but also traditional Maori beliefs and practices — among them cutting the heart from an enemy and offering it to the god Tu, and ritual cannibalism; although it is claimed that Titokowaru himself never ate human flesh.

Who were the 'Hauhaus'? In the early 1860s, Te Ua Haumene claimed to have visions, during which the Angel Gabriel had spoken to him. As a result he founded Pai Marire, translated as 'good and peaceful'. Along with other Maori nineteenth-century prophets, he compared the suffering of Maori under Europeans with the suffering of the Israelites under the Egyptians. He believed Maori should recover their ancestral land and be rid of the Pakeha. It was not unknown for the Christian missionaries, in explaining how Adam and Eve were the universal parents, to describe Maori as a lost tribe of

Israelites. 'Pai Marire' and 'Hauhau' were words uttered at the end of their prayers, referring to the breath of life given by God.

Despite Te Ua Haumene's insistence on peace, the religion was preached in Taranaki, which had been a battleground since 1860, and many of the new adherents believed they could only recover their land by violence against the invading settlers. Some warriors believed that the religion gave them immunity from bullets and were ferocious in battle. Throughout his account of the Titokowaru campaign, Cowan and other commentators refer dismissively to Titokowaru and his men only as 'the Hauhaus', accentuating a claim that they were aggressive religious fanatics (which some of them were) but diminishing the factors of land confiscation and loss of political influence.

Typical of its time, the 1966 *Encyclopedia of New Zealand* referred to him in one instance as 'the Hauhau cannibal'. The encyclopedia's summing up of the 1868 campaign reads: 'Titokowaru, a Hauhau chief of Patea, fell foul of authority over some stolen horses, took up arms and defeated Colonel McDonnell's ill-disciplined forces at Te Ngutu-o-te-Manu (7 September 1868), when von Tempsky and nineteen others were killed. Whitmore attacked Titokowaru unsuccessfully at Moturoa (7 November), but later drove him back into the forests of the upper Waitara, where he lapsed into sudden quietude.'

Politicians, Taranaki settlers and newspapers of

the time told a different story and make it clear that Titokowaru was a much more interesting man than just the religious fanatic he was labelled. He established his headquarters at Te Ngutu-o-te-Manu, near Kaponga in south Taranaki, and developed a large village with fifty-plus houses and an extensive marae. He held a series of peace meetings there and sent envoys to the north of the province. He led a peace march from the colonial military base at Waihi, 10 kilometres north-west of what is now the south Taranaki town of Hawera. The marchers called at Patea and moved on to Whanganui and Pipiriki, on the east bank of the Whanganui River. Before the peace march left Camp Waihi, he was entertained in the officers' mess.

Pakeha settlers, predominantly English, had come late to Taranaki but by the mid-1860s, many had been there for more than twenty-five years and the desire to expand their settlement had gained momentum over time. To them, Maori settled in small groups on what was regarded as 'undeveloped' land was a waste of resources and its transmutation into their fenced-off pastoral ideal was as inevitable as it was desirable: a move towards a civilised idyll, an improvement even on 'Home'.

Titokowaru even conceded that some more Ngati Ruanui land could be given up but then, as confiscation continued, he began organising non-violent opposition, obstructing surveyors and settlers on disputed land. Confrontations became more and more tense.

These protests disturbed the colonial government and invited inevitable retaliation — as they were designed to. The early settlers may have seen Maori as superior savages and even admired their courage and endurance but they were, nevertheless, still seen as savages. Maori, increasingly as the years went by, saw only loss.

The first serious attack of the war came in July 1868 at Turuturumokai, near the camp at Waihi, where an uncompleted redoubt was saved from being wiped out by a surprise attack by Titokowaru's Ngati Ruanui warriors only at the last minute when reinforcements arrived. The Maori attackers lost three men but the seriously outnumbered garrison lost ten with six wounded. It was a humbling defeat so close to the militia camp, but worse was to come.

Thomas McDonnell, promoted to Lieutenant-Colonel the previous year, swore vengeance. He made two abortive attacks on Te Ngutu-o-te-Manu, during August. The first time he got lost in the driving winter rain which raised the rivers and made progress through the bush slow. Ten days later he arrived at the village with about a hundred troops, found most of the people were gathering food, burned down some of the houses but his force was pursued by warriors as it withdrew and suffered four killed and nine wounded.

McDonnell was brought up in the Hokianga and had gained his rank after serving only in the colony. He was fluent in Maori, boasted profound knowledge of Maori culture and had been with Chute on the 1866 blitz through the province. He had a similar, earned reputation for ruthlessness. By 1868, he had his own farm on confiscated land near Patea.

On 7 September, Titokowaru and about sixty men were ready and waiting for what McDonnell expected would be a surprise attack on Te Ngutu-o-te-Manu. Titokowaru was warned of the advancing force: three hundred and sixty constabulary and militia supported by Whanganui kupapa under the direct command of the tough and astute Te Keepa Te Rangihiwinui, known as Major Kemp. The kupapa moved around the pa to attack from the side but, tactically, Titokowaru had persuaded McDonnell by implication that a newly constructed palisade was the focal point of the defence and so the militia advanced to the attack. It came under withering cross-fire from rifle pits alongside the approaches.

McDonnell was forced to withdraw and was blamed afterwards for a premature retreat, which was really forced on him by Titokowaru's brilliant tactics. The defeat was so comprehensive it cost the lives of twenty-five, including five officers, and twenty-six were wounded. Cowan said the battle, 'so weakened the numbers and the morale of McDonnell's force that all the country northward of Patea was soon abandoned to the Hauhaus'.

Gustavus von Tempsky, a fiery, arrogant Prussian adventurer who had become a legendary figure in fighting Maori with his Forest Rangers, was killed in the battle.

Cowan wrote of the Maori celebration in the aftermath: 'On the ground lie the bodies of twenty white men, stripped by the Hauhaus, who had dragged them in from the forest where they had been left when the retreat began. Von Tempsky's body is there . . .

'The camp is in a fury of exultation over the fall of "Manu-rau" ("Many birds"), the name given to him because of his activity in guerrilla warfare; von Tempsky was as nimble as the birds of the forest. And there, in front of the heap of slain, stands Titokowaru, the planner of ambuscades and midnight surprises, the victor of Te Ngutu-o-te-Manu . . . At last he raises his head, and in a great croaking voice cries to his men that they must tahutahu the bodies of the pakehas — they must destroy them by fire.'

The settlers could not accept that Maori had out-thought and out-fought the militia and so McDonnell's retreat was a point of blame. He returned it in a vituperative fury, writing letters to the government in his defence. But he was dismissed and replaced by the shrewd, experienced and deeply disliked Lieutenant-Colonel George Whitmore. Whitmore, used by the government in both the campaigns against Titokowaru and Te Kooti, moved across the country as the two generals continued to gain control over large areas of the North Island.

The new Governor, George Bowen, put a bounty of £1000 on Titokowaru's head as he and his warriors moved quickly to the south over land vacated by the retreating government force, gathering strength as they went. His success attracted supporters from other hapu in the region, although he was still heavily outnumbered by the men under Whitmore, based at Patea. He retorted by placing a bounty of two shillings and sixpence on the governor's head.

Titokowaru began to build a defensive pa at Moturoa, near present-day Waverley, and in early November Whitmore went on to the attack with two hundred and fifty constabulary and three hundred Whanganui Maori led by Te Keepa. The pa appeared to be unfinished as Whitmore divided his forces into three with the kupapa in reserve and Whitmore in close back-up of the attacking party led by a veteran of Turuturumokai, Major William Hunter.

What they didn't anticipate was a sophisticated two-level firing trench and three towers of packed earth. The Maori defenders held their fire until the attackers were closing in and then cut them down. They then swiftly occupied disguised rifle pits on the flanks of Whitmore's supporting group and their withering fire forced him to retreat. Nineteen were killed and twenty wounded in the brief battle. Titokowaru lost one man.

Over the summer of 1868–69, South Taranaki was his. His followers had swelled from the original sixty to a thousand from Taranaki iwi. He was building a pa at Tauranga-ika. A Kingite force from the Waikato moved into north Taranaki and attacked the Pukearuhe redoubt near New Plymouth. The government was so embroiled with

Titokowaru and with the guerrilla Te Kooti Arikirangi on the East Coast, it discussed abandoning self-government, for the time being at least, and applying to the Colonial Office for the return of British troops. It even raised the possibility of returning all confiscated land.

Then it all went away. Titokowaru somehow lost his mana and his army melted away before any battle for Tauranga-ika could take place. What caused this desperate retreat is not really known. Reasons given by historians include that he ran out of food or ammunition, or both, or that he sensed his defences would be overwhelmed by a large, cautious and determined enemy. Most, however, believe he had a sexual liaison with the wife of one of his senior allied chiefs and that destroyed his mana and caused his men to desert him. The government and settlers agreed to let him go but he left behind a lingering sense of menace that held back settler confiscations for most of a decade.

The story of Titokowaru does not end there. He built a village at Okaiawa, his birthplace, between Mt Taranaki and the coast and developed a profitable business growing and selling cocksfoot grass seed. Then, in 1880, a government report noted that the 'natives' had started pulling up pegs near Okaiawa after a surveyor set up a road line 'where it cut into a large fenced enclosure, sown with English cocksfoot grass, a yearly source of income . . .

'This unlucky step,' the report continued, 'alienated Titokowaru and lost us the benefit of his friendly influence [but] there was a far more widespread cause of dissatisfaction influencing the whole body of natives . . . This was the omission of the government to make proper reserves for them.'

The report added that 'reserves' had never been marked on the ground and that 'not even those marked on the plan were ever made known to the natives'.

Such a direct, provocative challenge to Maori agricultural existence could not be ignored. However, Titokowaru had resumed his peace mode and it was reinforced this time by the historically famous passive resisters, Erueti Te Whiti o Rongomai III and Tohu Kakahi at nearby Parihaka. They not only pulled surveyor's pegs, they ploughed land in dispute. As one commentator wrote: 'Te Whiti and Tohu deliberated policy, and Titokowaru carried it out.'

But it was the preternatural calm of Te Whiti that guaranteed that peaceful resistance would hold. He was a mystic whose speeches were oracular with abstruse religious allusions and colourful metaphors. The protesters continued to obstruct the surveyors and accepted mass arrests. An exasperated government made its move at the end of 1881 when the Native Minister, John Bryce, invaded Parihaka. A truculent Whanganui farmer turned politician, he had been a lieutenant in a militia earlier in the Taranaki conflict.

There was some support for the Parihaka Maori and it was known that the Governor Sir Arthur Gordon, who was out of the country, was sympathetic, but it was not enough to curb the government of Premier John Hall, a Canterbury sheep farmer.

The population of Parihaka at the time was estimated at around two thousand, with growth from its inception in the mid-1860s helped by refugees from confiscated land. Although the government's commissioners on Taranaki issues, William Fox and Francis Dillon Bell, had said 'the West Coast question would never be settled without some arrangement with Te Whiti', Bryce was contemptuous of the Maori leader. He said Te Whiti's 'pretensions to supernatural powers were enormous' and it was 'probable that he, occasionally at least, believed in his own pretensions'. G. W. Rusden, in his 1895 *History of New Zealand*, said Bryce regarded the Maori pacifist leader as 'a blight on the minds of the natives' that he wanted to remove.

The government, having decided that it needed to halt the continuing protests, instructed Bryce to close Parihaka down. He personally, on horseback, headed a force of about sixteen hundred constabulary called in from all over the North Island with the implied glory of an army defending its country from intransigent savages. The force was wary of a trap — perhaps to be sprung by Titokowaru — when it entered the village at dawn on 5 November 1881. They were met by hundreds of singing, skipping children offering food. Had any Maori fired shots there could have been a massacre but they remained steady in their pacifism as the soldiers destroyed the village and dispersed its inhabitants.

Te Whiti, Tohu and Titokowaru were arrested and sent to jail without trial. Bryce might have carried the day but the three Maori leaders have carried the years as history has made Parihaka a symbol of gallant, non-violent resistance to the oppression of a government in the hands of land-hungry immigrants. There was, though, a measure of contempt for the government and Bryce expressed in newspapers soon after the raid. Although Bryce had taken some trouble to keep the Press away, reporters had sneaked into Parihaka and the public and politicians quickly learnt what had happened.

As the years went by, contumely increased, perhaps summed up by a satirical poem by Jessie Mackay, a nationally known poet who was seventeen at the time of the Parihaka raid. It is called 'The Charge at Parihaka' and was a take on 'The Charge of the Light Brigade', the great poem by Alfred, Lord Tennyson. Mackay's verse was revived in Bill Manhire's 1993 anthology, *100 New Zealand Poems*, and again in Harvey McQueen's *My Favourite New Zealand Poems* in 2010:

The Charge at Parihaka

Yet a league, yet a league
Yet a league onward
Straight to the Maori Pah
Marched the Twelve Hundred.

'Forward the Volunteers!
Is there a man who fears?'
Over the ferny plain
Marched the Twelve Hundred.

'Forward!' the Colonel said;
Was there a man dismayed?
No, for the heroes knew
There was no danger
Theirs not to reckon why
Theirs not to bleed or die,
Theirs but to trample by:
Each dauntless ranger.

Pressmen to right of them,
Pressmen to left of them,
Pressmen in front of them,
Chuckled and wondered.
Dreading their country's eyes,
Long was the search and wise,
Vain, for the pressmen five
Had, by a slight device,
Foiled the Twelve Hundred.

Gleamed all their muskets bare,
Fright'ning the children there,
Heroes to do and dare,
Charging a village, while

Maoridom wondered.
Plunged in potato fields,
Honour to hunger yields.
Te Whiti and Tohu
Bearing not swords or shields,
Questioned nor wondered,
Calmly before them sat;
Faced the Twelve Hundred.

Children to right of them,
Children to left of them,
Women in front of them,
Saw them and wondered;
Stormed at with jeer and groan,
Foiled by the five alone,
Never was a trumpet blown
O'er such a deed of arms.
Back with their captives three
Taken so gallantly,
Rode the Twelve Hundred.

When can their glory fade?
Oh! The wild charge they made,
New Zealand wondered
Whether each doughty soul,
Paid for the pigs he stole:
Noble Twelve Hundred.

— Jessie Mackay

At the time Titokowaru was gaining control of southern Taranaki, Te Kooti Arikirangi Te Turuki was causing havoc in Poverty Bay and the Bay of Plenty. Te Kooti, a member of the Poverty Bay Rongowhakaata people (Ngati Maru), became legendary as a guerrilla fighter with his relatively small band of men in the bush, the bogeyman of the settlers on the east coast of the North Island.

Poverty Bay — known to Maori as Turanganui-a-kiwa — was the second place in New Zealand to have an English name, after Young Nicks Head. When James Cook arrived there in 1769 after the long voyage from the Society Islands he was unable to get any of the sort of supplies he and his crew needed, except some herbs to defeat scurvy, and gave the name in frustration. In fact, the alluvial plain in Poverty Bay is one of the most fertile in New Zealand, producing high-value vegetables, fruit and wine. From early in the twentieth century the economy of the region has been bolstered further by sheep farming on the surrounding hill country, and pine plantations.

The first Pakeha traders set up shop near Gisborne in the 1830s, when Maori began trading wheat and potatoes. European settlers had moved on to the plain by the time of Te Kooti in the 1860s.

Although fighting at local level across the central North Island had not really stopped in the period after the major battles of the early 1860s, those Maori forces actively confronting colonial militia and kupapa had no success. In Hawke's Bay, Ngati Porou had been subdued by militia and Arawa kupapa. The Waerenga-a-Hika pa close to Gisborne had been stormed and the Maori 'rebels' retreated to Waikaremoana. Skirmishes continued through the region as Maori continued to resent and resist land confiscations.

After the Waikato War, the King movement lost its ability to organise and support beleaguered hapu. In many cases the tactic of the militia, as it had been in Taranaki, was to attack Maori villages and destroy crops, storage installations and homes, crippling them economically. So Te Kooti's striking victories concentrated the mind of local and national government.

He was educated at William Williams' Anglican mission school near present-day Gisborne, acquired a detailed knowledge of the Scriptures from the Maori Bible, as many bright young Maori did with the well-honed memories of people from oral cultures. His early ambition to become a lay preacher was blunted by the truculent, philandering and lawless behaviour on the part of himself and some young associates, offending Pakeha and Maori leaders alike. He became a competent sailor and was involved in cut-price trade between Poverty Bay and Auckland, using Maori-owned vessels, which helped alienate him from Pakeha traders.

In 1865, Te Kooti took part, on the government side, in an attack on Pai Marire forces defending the fortified Waerenga-a-Hika pa against militia and kupapa. After the pa fell, about two hundred of the Hauhau captives were dispatched to prison in the Chatham Islands, or Wharekauri as Maori called it. It was with them that Te Kooti, then in his mid-to-late thirties, was also exiled. He was accused of being an anti-government spy. He was released after a first arrest but arrested again and never given any kind of trial, despite an appeal to Provincial Superintendent Donald McLean.

James Cowan wrote: 'There is no doubt that several Gisborne people thought that Te Kooti was a troublesome fellow who would be better out of the way, and the opportunity to send him off to Wharekauri was too good to be missed.' Among those who wanted him out of the way were senior Maori, too often personally affected by Te Kooti's sexual promiscuity.

Captain Gilbert Mair, the Pakeha commander of the famous Arawa Flying Column that fought on the government side, often against Te Kooti, said later: 'So far as Te Kooti's guilt was concerned, I am perfectly certain that no charge could have been sustained against him in any court of competent jurisdiction prior to his deportation to the Chathams.'

Placing Te Kooti in exile proved to be an egregious mistake by the government because it was during his two years on Wharekauri that he developed his new religion of Ringatu (the Upraised Hand) and gained impressive mana and ultimately unchallenged leadership of the exiles.

Ringatu sprang from what Te Kooti described as visions during bouts of fever. 'The Spirit of God,' he claimed, raised him from unconsciousness. He held religious services in darkened rooms during which he used phosphorous and legerdemain to show flames shooting from his upraised hand. Over the years he devised his ritual, using Old Testament texts and the Pai Marire theme of Maori being deprived of their own country in the manner of the ancient Israelites. Each morning, according to reports, he called his people to karakia, and psalms were sung, usually 32 and 34.

Te Kooti was not a big man, about 170 centimetres, according to one report, and wiry rather than muscular. His strength was his iron will and the decisiveness and determination that attracted followers. Posing as a prophet, even a god, he gained deep loyalty from his fellow exiles and devised a complex plan, brilliantly executed, to escape and return to Poverty Bay.

The prisoners had been told their sentence would be two years but that time came and went, although some senior chiefs had been returned to the mainland. When a supply ship arrived from Wellington — the three-masted schooner, *Rifleman* — it was taken over by Te Kooti and his acolytes. Men, women and children, in all two hundred and ninety-eight of them, were smuggled aboard. Another smaller vessel was also captured but then wrecked on the coast. One guard at the port was killed but the crew and other guards were treated well and, according to a pre-arrangement, set free on arrival at Whareongaonga, south of Gisborne.

The journey was arduous — the flight of the Israelites from bondage, as he later described it. Strong westerlies meant the *Rifleman* had to return to port after a day and then struggled to sail across the wind for three days as Te Kooti worried about a government steamer arriving. He ordered his followers to sacrifice their precious belongings, their taonga, by discarding them overboard as a sacrifice. He also had Te Warihi Potini, his uncle, whom he suspected of being a spy and a non-believer, thrown over the side of the ship. When conditions changed for the better, he persuaded his fellow travellers that it was because of the sacrifices and his prayers for divine intervention.

When they arrived back in Poverty Bay in July 1868, the renegades were well supplied with arms, ammunition, money and supplies that they had taken from Wharekauri or were aboard the supply ship when they took control. The loot was considerable: an estimated £522 in cash, a range of rifles and revolvers, plus ammunition as well as tonnes of flour, sugar and other foodstuffs.

The *Rifleman* was released and the captain chose to set sail for the ship's home port of Wellington rather than to nearby Gisborne to raise the alarm. Nevertheless, the authorities learnt of the escape soon enough and Resident Magistrate at Gisborne Captain Reginald Biggs sent a Maori emissary to demand the escapees surrender their arms. They refused. From then on, the mistrust was mutual and Te Kooti embarked on his extraordinary military career.

He had announced in Wharekauri that he had created the new religion for Maori and, when back in Poverty Bay, said he simply wanted to move in peace into the King Country to challenge King Tawhiao, who had embraced Pai Marire, for spiritual leadership of the Maori people. He had by this time developed a well-shaped religion with special waiata and forms and times of worship. He had, he told the emissary, no fight with the government. But Captain Biggs decided Te Kooti and his party had to be stopped at Paparatu and their progress blocked. That was the pattern of the encounters to come — the militia trying to catch and defeat him in his journey. They failed.

At Paparatu, on 20 July, the first encounter of the campaign, Te Kooti isolated the pursuing militia, surrounded them and forced them to retreat raggedly, carrying their dead and wounded, down from the hills to the open country below. He didn't pursue them but captured their supply base and their horses. Similarly, at Te Koneke four days later and at Ruakituri on 8 August he inflicted a defeat on another force of militia attempting to halt his progress towards an old established pa at Puketapu, near Lake Waikaremoana. They were fighting over difficult terrain which, if Te Kooti didn't know, he had warriors with him who certainly did.

At Puketapu, the group shored up the defences of an already strong pa and waited for replies from the King Country and from Tuhoe for permission to enter their territory. Tawhiao replied that his forces would be repelled and Tuhoe also refused entry, but with some equivocation. Te Kooti also sent emissaries to Poverty Bay Maori (including his own Rongowhakaata hapu), and to Bay of Plenty, Taupo and Urewera people and the mighty Ngati Kahungunu seeking support in a bid to re-take the land and the mana they had lost to Pakeha. The chance of victory at that time must have been obvious enough but any response was confined to a few individuals from two hapu. 'Sympathy and passive support' was offered, wrote James Belich, but war weariness suppressed any desire for military support. There were, though, Ngati Kahungunu and Ngati Maniapoto warriors, and some from other iwi among his troops.

The government had decided to make a genuine peace offer to Te Kooti and his party while he was at Puketapu, offering them pardons and an allocation of land if they would give up their arms. It's doubtful he ever received any kind of formal proposition and, if he did, it would have taken a leap of trust for him to have accepted it. He rested up at Puketapu to heal a foot wound he had received at Ruakituri.

Whatever were the persuasive factors, Te Kooti had decided to stop running, to postpone, at least for the meantime, any move against Tawhiao or any attempt to establish his religion in the Ureweras. He would go it alone.

Governor Grey had gone three years before and with him went the British army and the strong executive power he had wielded against what was now a newly empowered colonial government in Wellington. Any defence against Maori intransigence had to be conducted by kupapa and settler militia, whose strength and efficiency were being sorely tested in Taranaki. Te Kooti's next move in the context of panic spread by Titokowaru shook the confidence of the young colony. He invaded Poverty Bay. His attack was a surprise in both its direction and its timing.

The government had considered for some time the possibility of an attack on Poverty Bay and had made tentative plans for defence. A rumour spread by Te Kooti's men or his allies was that he would move against the northern Hawke's Bay town of Wairoa, where the garrison was quickly strengthened. Similar misinformation convinced Captain Biggs that if an attack came it would be from the south and he arranged defences accordingly. If Biggs didn't know where Te Kooti was, Te Kooti knew very well what Biggs's dispositions were.

During October, he worked his way north into country very familiar to him and attacked from the west, after moving cautiously along old Maori tracks, having to clear some of the growth to get the horses through. Spring would soon give way to the balm of summer over the Poverty Bay plain.

Just before midnight, on 9 November, Te Kooti dispatched 'kokiri', striking parties of warriors, like posses of cavalry. They moved quickly and mercilessly across the plain into settlers' properties, killing families and burning houses. Under his direction civilians — women and children as well as non-combatant men — were executed, more Maori than Pakeha, and in one case women and children were cut down because God had told him it needed to be done. Among the first victims was Biggs.

This was the supreme arrogance of a man who had come to think of himself as the hand of god. He is said to have declared on making his decision to invade: 'God would give the Turanganui country, and all the best places of the Europeans, back to him and his people.'

But it was also utu on a grand scale for the injustices inflicted upon him since his exile without trial and for the unremitting harassment since his arrival back from Wharekauri. It was utu that motivated him on 12 November when he went to Oweta pa in response to an invitation by Paratene Pototi who had three years before mocked him as he was put aboard the prison ship that took him into exile. The unarmed Paratene and six other chiefs were executed on the spot. If numbers were counted, local Maori were the main victims of the campaign.

The speed and ruthlessness of Te Kooti's warriors split the fearful enemy into defensive factions, although some of them fought with determination and gallantry. He also spread fear among the civilian population as it fled to the safety of the Turanganui (Gisborne) redoubt from where women and children were evacuated to Napier. A number of settlers cut off from the redoubt were taken off by sea from near Mahia.

That night and the following two days were terrifying and traumatic for the locals who were left to care for themselves where they could. Those who survived the immediate onslaught fled to the redoubt or to the coast as Te Kooti's forces operated virtually without opposition. James Cowan wrote: 'The plain was ablaze with burning homes, and the blood-maddened Hauhaus were galloping over the country, shooting indiscriminately, looting and destroying'. It clearly wasn't as indiscriminate as Cowan says, and he still uses the pejorative 'Hauhaus'. Te Kooti stayed in control of Poverty Bay for about ten terrifying days.

As settler reinforcements from Napier and kupapa quickly gathered to respond, he set out for a formidable stronghold, Ngatapa, laden with huge quantities of looted arms and ammunition, horses and food supplies. He was accompanied by a large number of new recruits to his cause, and they were slowed down by the hundreds of women and children in his party.

But Ngatapa was the beginning of the end for Te Kooti even though it was a few years before his demise. At Makaretu, on the way, he was caught up by a large kupapa force, which held its ground against counter-attacks and waited for ammunition to be replenished from a store at Patutahi. The force was large enough and determined enough to have overwhelmed Te Kooti, who had already lost a lot of men, but he pulled off one of the striking guerrilla coups for which he had become infamous. He dispatched twenty of his top horsemen on a lightning raid to Patutahi where they confiscated the ammunition for themselves.

Even then, his escape to the temporary safety of Ngatapa was a narrow one, and if assaulting the pa was a seriously difficult project for the forces besieging it, they were assembling the numbers and the resources to try. The defenders would have been able to hold out the attackers for some time — except for the lack of access to water for about seven hundred people which meant their stay was essentially short term. On 5 January, the beleaguered population slid down the 18-metre-high cliff at the rear of the pa on ropes made of vines. The ruse was noticed soon enough and although many escaped into the bush, including Te Kooti, hundreds were captured.

What followed established that Pakeha were not immune to vengeance: more than a hundred male prisoners were summarily executed under orders from Major Rapata Wahawaha of Ngati Porou — but with the connivance of Colonel Whitmore, the senior officer, and the Minister of Native Affairs, James C. Richmond, of the Taranaki Richmond family, who were both present. Although they stopped the killing of women and children, they turned their backs when it came to the executions of the captured men.

Te Kooti and those loyal to him who escaped fled to

the depths of the hill country between Poverty Bay and the Ureweras where they stayed for a few months before moving on into the Ureweras. The Tuhoe people — disaffected by the confiscation of some of their land on the Bay of Plenty edge of their domain and distrustful of the government — were persuaded to accept his leadership as a prophet and military commander. Striking from the fastness of the high, broken country he attacked a number of Maori communities on the coast inflicting heavy casualties among Maori he considered were aligned with the government. In March 1869, he led his men on a raid into Whakatane, besieging the pa, and looting and burning the village. He was in the district for nearly a week but retreated into the hills before a force of Arawa arrived, led by their famous commander Major Gilbert Mair.

His next foray was across Lake Waikaremoana to Mohaka, which local intelligence advised him would be undefended. More than sixty people, Maori and Pakeha, were mercilessly killed and the town looted and burned. A party of about a hundred Ngati Kahungunu marched to the rescue but were ambushed and forced to retreat before Te Kooti and his men escaped.

Tuhoe had long lived as an isolated people, safe in their inaccessible mountainous tribal land. Their remoteness was a barrier to other Maori in the region long wary of any invasion of such broken country the locals knew so well. Ethnologist Elsdon Best called Tuhoe 'The Children of the Mist' because of their distinctive genealogical tradition that their forebears sprang from the heavens and the mountains themselves. Such romantic stuff was of no value to a government that wanted to catch or kill Te Kooti.

It was for Whitmore, back from Taranaki, to launch a high-risk invasion in a bid to stop Te Kooti and crush his new-found followers. Native Minister Richmond and Whitmore put together an army for the campaign of more than six hundred men of the constabulary, backed by five hundred and sixty Arawa kupapa. It failed in that Te Kooti escaped to Taupo and then the King Country but Whitmore's three-pronged attack and a later invasion by Te Arawa, Ngati Kahungunu and Ngati Porou inflicted terrible damage on the economy of Tuhoe.

It says much of Te Kooti's powers of persuasion that he received sympathy and some support from both Rewi Maniapoto and Tawhiao, but it was short-lived. He was pursued around the Taupo region, moved back briefly into the Ureweras but he was gradually losing support and only narrowly escaped both constabulary and kupapa. In 1872, he moved into the King Country, protected by Tawhiao until he was finally pardoned by the government in 1883. He died ten years later, a shell of a man no longer capable of commanding respect let alone awe.

Cowan wrote in the 1920s that when he met Te Kooti four years before he died 'he was not an impressive figure: a bowed rather undersized man, prematurely aged, with a straggly white beard; he was very much reduced in health by his terribly arduous campaigning life and also by his intemperate habits. His features were well cut, his nose aquiline, dominating, his eyes very keen and searching . . . '

It is hard to feel as much sympathy for Te Kooti as it is for many of the other Maori leaders who fought so valiantly to retain or regain their land and their rangatiratanga, for the right to hold onto some of the more important values of their long cultural tradition. With Te Kooti there is always the sense that his high intelligence and brilliant skill as a guerrilla general were mostly in the service of self, of a man who believed, for most of his life at least, that he was the messiah and would ruthlessly exploit anyone who refused to follow him and accept the semi-divine image he held of himself.

Epilogue:
The Maori Revival

*T*he Maori revival that gained momentum in the 1970s confronted New Zealanders with their history for the first time in a century.

This regeneration of Maori activism has brought incremental recognition over the past forty years of historic abuses of the Treaty of Waitangi and government attempts to acknowledge and redress them. For the first time, on 28 October 2017, what is to become an official New Zealand Wars Day recognises the arduous and courageous fight by Maori in the defence of their land and mana through almost three decades from the 1840s.

The seeds of the Maori revival were planted when many young Maori moved into the cities after the Second World War. During this period the government was rearranging land ownership in a way that would make acquisition easier by non-Maori. Young urban Maori began to talk about the Treaty of Waitangi and historic abuses of its provisions that had dispossessed them over more than a century.

Early in the 1970s, I was working some evenings with a charity in the centre of Auckland and some Nga Tamatoa (Young Warriors) had an office in the same building. They were loud and funny, and definitely not to be messed with. They were dismissed as 'Maori radicals' even by conservative Maori elders after they disrupted Waitangi Day in 1971 and 1972; but they were far from done. Among them were Tame Iti (Tuhoe) and Rawiri Paratene (Ngapuhi).

I learnt something from Paratene about attitudes towards Maori. In 1983, he was the Burns Fellow with an office on the campus at Otago University in Dunedin. I travelled down to interview him for a television programme.

A widespread series of protests were happening on the campus at the time and the police were out in force. When we left his office after the interview we went down in the lift to the basement together. He walked one way and I went another. I was a reasonably formally dressed Pakeha. He was a Maori dressed casually. I walked out past the police who barely noticed me, but he was stopped and questioned. I walked over to him but he waved me away. Since then this cool and gracious writer/ actor has travelled the world acting in Globe Theatre Shakespearean productions.

Conservative tribal elders didn't approve at first of Nga Tamatoa but they also carried a sense of having been wronged during a past covered up for Pakeha consumption, and quite quickly that sense moved into the mainstream.

By 1975, disaffection about continuing loss of land among increasing numbers of people inspired a 79-year-old Northland kuia (elder) Whina Cooper to set off from Te Hapua in Northland on a thousand-kilometre protest hikoi (communal march) to Wellington. On arrival, she was joined by about five thousand people in the grounds of Parliament and presented a petition carrying sixty thousand signatures to Prime Minister Bill Rowling.

The mood that the abuses of the past needed to be addressed was spreading. The Waitangi Tribunal was born and began to grow.

Two years after the hikoi, Ngati Whatua occupied Bastion Point, a superb piece of land with an elevated view of the Waitemata that developers had coveted for a long time. An Auckland businessman a few years before had shown me the plans for an international hotel he wanted to build there one day. He was waiting.

The land had been given to the nation by Ngati Whatua as a defensive position during the nineteenth century 'Russian scare': the paranoid fear that the Russians would invade us when they were at war with Britain. But rather than return it at last, the government decided to sell it for luxury housing.

Bastion Point became a focal point for historical Maori grievances. Ngati Whatua, supported by some Pakeha, occupied the land and camped on it. They stayed there for more than five hundred days. The government, led by Robert Muldoon, not untypically, sent the police in to arrest the protestors and demolish their makeshift shelters. But public opinion had turned in favour of the protestors. The luxury houses were never built, and the land was returned to Ngati Whatua ten years later.

The Waitangi Tribunal has advanced steadily after a start in 1975 that required it to look only at recent land losses. In 1985, it was charged with investigating land confiscation abuses back to 1840 and it was helped greatly by the Jim Bolger government of the 1990s and Douglas Graham, who became Minister in Charge of Treaty Negotiations in 1991. Graham was an eloquent spokesman for the relevance of our history as the great-grandson of pioneer Robert Graham who arrived in Auckland aboard the *Jane Gifford* in 1842 and played a significant part in national politics and the early development of the tourist industry.

Since the1990s, successive governments have continued to co-operate with the Waitangi Tribunal as it unravels injustices and attempts to make redress. It has been a long haul for a nation that suffered so long from historical amnesia to, at last, achieve a positive acknowledgement — through a day set aside each year — of the importance of the New Zealand Wars to our past and their impact on our present.

Selected reading

There is a huge amount of literature about Maori and Pakeha history, most of it written since the 1980s. For those who want to dive deeply into the issue the basic texts are:

Anderson, A., Binney, J., Harris, A. *Tangata Whenua: An Illustrated History* (Bridget Williams Books, Wellington, 2015). This brilliant, accessible book has contributions from Vincent O'Malley and Alan Ward.

Belich, James. *I Shall Not Die: Titokowaru's War, New Zealand, 1868–9* (Allen & Unwin/Port Nicholson Press, Wellington, 1989)

Belich, James. *The New Zealand Wars and the Victorian Interpretation of Racial Conflict* (Auckland University Press, Auckland, 1986. Expanded and reissued in 2015.) An essential text for anyone deeply interested in the wars.

Cowan, James. *The New Zealand Wars: A history of the Maori campaigns and the pioneering period*. Two volumes first published in 1922 and reissued in 1955 by the Government Printer, Wellington.

Crosby, Ron. *Kupapa: The bitter legacy of Maori alliances with the crown* (Penguin Random House New Zealand, Auckland, 2015)

Gorst, John Eldon. *The Maori King* (Paul's Book Arcade, 1959; reprinted from the Macmillan edition of 1864)

King, Michael. *Whina: A biography of Whina Cooper* (Hodder & Stoughton, Auckland, 1983).

Lee, Jack. *I Have Named It the Bay of Islands . . .* (Hodder & Stoughton, Auckland, 1983)

Metge, Joan. *The Maoris of New Zealand* (Routledge & Keegan Paul, London, 1967)

Moon, Paul. *Fatal Frontiers: A new history of New Zealand in the decade before the treaty* (Penguin Books, Auckland, 2006)

Moon, Paul. *FitzRoy: Governor in crisis, 1848–1845* (David Ling Publishing Ltd, Auckland, 2000)

O'Malley, Vincent. *The Great War for New Zealand: Waikato 1800–2000* (Bridget Williams Books, Wellington, 2016)

Orange, Claudia. *An Illustrated History of the Treaty of Waitangi* (Bridget Williams Books, Wellington, 2003)

Sinclair, Keith. *Kinds of Peace: Maori people after the Wars 1870–85* (Auckland University Press, Auckland, 1991)

Sinclair, Keith. *The Origins of the Maori Wars* (New Zealand University Press, Wellington, 1957)

Ward, Alan. *A Show of Justice: Racial 'amalgamation' in nineteenth century New Zealand* (Australian National University Press, Canberra, 1974)

Index

The author

Gordon McLauchlan is a highly regarded author, journalist and social commentator, writing for newspapers and magazines both locally and internationally, and publishing many books. His specific areas of interest are the historical, social and political heritage of New Zealanders, literature, agriculture, tourism and media.

In the course of his journalistic career he has worked as a senior reporter, sportswriter and sub-editor on provincial and regional newspapers, as well as for the New Zealand Broadcasting Service and the New Zealand Press Association. Since the mid-1970s he has been a freelance writer, broadcaster and public affairs consultant, including nine years as an investigative reporter for the *National Business Review*, and as books editor of the *New Zealand Herald* for which he also wrote a weekly op-ed column for thirty years.

A generalist with a wide range of interests, McLauchlan has a substantial private reference library, which was well utilised when he edited and wrote much of Bateman's *New Zealand Encyclopedia*, and compiled the 2000 New Zealand questions for Trivial Pursuit as well as the questions for the first two seasons of the television programme, *Sale of the Century*.

He has had a long association with the New Zealand Society of Authors (PEN NZ Inc.), including a two-year stint as president (1995–96), and also as the New Zealand delegate at International PEN congresses in Edinburgh, Helsinki, Warsaw and Moscow. In addition, he was the founding president of the Travel Communicators of New Zealand (Travcom); the founding chair of the Michael King Writers' Studio Trust; was a trustee of the Frank Sargeson Trust for twenty years; and took over as editor of the New Zealand Automobile Association's *Directions* magazine from 1998–99.

McLauchlan served as a Wattie Book of the Year judge in 1978 and convener in 1979; a Montana National Book Awards judge in 1998 and convener in 1999; and was a director for seven years (three of them as chairman) of Copyright Licensing Limited (now Copyright Licensing New Zealand) which controls licences and revenue for copyright holders and publishers.

Gordon's other publications include:
Great Tales from Rural New Zealand (David Bateman Ltd, 2016)

Great Tales from New Zealand History (re-released by David Bateman Ltd, 2014)

A Short History of New Zealand (new edition, David Bateman Ltd, 2014)

The Passionless People Revisited (David Bateman Ltd, 2012 — *The Passionless People*, a best-selling social commentary on New Zealanders was originally published in 1976)

The Saltwater Highway (David Bateman Ltd, 2012)

The New Zealand Encyclopedia (1984, revised 1987, 1991, revised and expanded 1995)

The Farming of New Zealand, a history of New Zealand agriculture (1981), and many others.

He has also edited and contributed to a number of highly successful short story anthologies, hosted and presented television programmes and, since 2011, has been a regular panel member on Jim Mora's afternoon RNZ programme.